James Candish

The epistle of Paul to the Ephesians

James Candish

The epistle of Paul to the Ephesians

ISBN/EAN: 9783337729851

Printed in Europe, USA, Canada, Australia, Japan

Cover: Foto ©ninafisch / pixelio.de

More available books at **www.hansebooks.com**

HANDBOOKS

FOR

BIBLE CLASSES

AND PRIVATE STUDENTS

EDITED BY

PROFESSOR MARCUS DODS, D.D.

AND

REV. ALEXANDER WHYTE, D.D.

THE EPISTLE OF PAUL TO THE EPHESIANS

EDINBURGH
T. & T. CLARK, 38 GEORGE STREET
1895

THE EPISTLE OF PAUL

TO

THE EPHESIANS

With Introduction and Notes

BY

JAMES S. CANDLISH, D.D.
PROFESSOR OF THEOLOGY, FREE CHURCH COLLEGE, GLASGOW

———◆———

EDINBURGH
T. & T. CLARK, 38 GEORGE STREET
1895

CONTENTS

INTRODUCTION

	PAGE
I. AUTHORSHIP	11
II. TO WHOM ADDRESSED	13
III. TIME AND CIRCUMSTANCES OF WRITING	16
IV. SCOPE AND CONTENTS OF THE LETTER	21
V. RELATION OF THE EPISTLE TO OTHER PARTS OF THE NEW TESTAMENT	23

THE EPISTLE WITH NOTES

THE SALUTATION. CH. I. 1, 2	31
PRAISE FOR GOD'S SALVATION. CH. I. 3-14	33
PRAYER FOR BELIEVERS. CH. I. 15-II. 10	44
REMINDER OF THEIR CHANGED POSITION. CH. II. 11-22	59
APPEAL AS THE PRISONER OF CHRIST FOR THE GENTILES. CH. III. 1-21	66
EXHORTATION TO LOVING UNITY. CH. IV. 1-16.	81
EXHORTATION TO CHRISTIAN LIVING. CH. IV. 17-V. 21	93
EXHORTATION TO MUTUAL SUBJECTION. CH. V. 22-VI. 9	111
CALL TO ARMS AGAINST SPIRITUAL FOES. CH. VI. 10-20	122
CONCLUSION. CH. VI. 21-24	129

THE EPISTLE OF PAUL TO THE EPHESIANS

INTRODUCTION

I. AUTHORSHIP

THE Epistle is written in the name of the Apostle Paul, in the form in which letters were usually composed in ancient times, beginning with a sentence in which the author gave his name in a greeting, or expression of good wishes to those to whom he was sending it. The form of the greeting, too, is that which Paul uses in his admittedly genuine epistles; and it is a characteristic one, not a mere standing form, nor even the same as in other New Testament epistles. These facts afford a strong presumption that it is really the work of the apostle. This is the most simple and natural explanation: if it is not true, it is hard to avoid the conclusion, that there has been a deliberate attempt to pass off as Paul's a writing not really his, and the high moral tone of the epistle is against this.

The profession of the epistle itself is also confirmed by a large body of external evidence, *i.e.* by the testimony of later writers, that it existed in their days and was acknowledged to be genuine. It has been read, expounded, and quoted as Paul's by a series of writers that can be traced back without a break to Irenæus, who was a native of Asia Minor, the district to which it professes to have been sent, in the second century. His teacher Polycarp, who was a disciple of the Apostle John, and was Bishop of Smyrna, uses words from it as Scripture in his Epistle to the Philippians; and it is referred to in the letters ascribed to Ignatius in the early part of the second century. While there were different opinions in the early Church as to those to whom the epistle was addressed, there never was any doubt or question that it was written by Paul, till the present century.

The body of testimony in its favour is at least as strong as is usually deemed sufficient for documents of such antiquity, and has satisfied most scholars; but in modern times a certain school of critics, carrying to an extreme their doubts about the early Christian writings, have rejected this epistle, as not by Paul himself, but by some of his disciples. Their suspicions are grounded entirely on internal evidence, *i.e.* on what the epistle itself contains. Now, arguments of this kind are sometimes the most convincing proof of a writing not being genuine, when it can be shown to contain words, or references to facts, that are later than its professed date. It is like circumstantial evidence in criminal cases, which is most conclusive when without a flaw; but as that, when not perfect, has often led to the condemnation of the innocent, so internal evidence has not seldom occasioned the rejection of really genuine books. In this case the grounds of suspicion are not at all of a definite and tangible kind,—no reference, for example, to the destruction of Jerusalem, or to the persecution of the Christians by the Romans; and no use of words or phrases that are certainly later than the time of Paul: only, it is thought, that the contents and style of the epistle are unlike those of Paul's genuine letters, and bear traces of later forms of thought; and that the resemblance of this epistle to that to the Colossians is such, that it must have been copied from it in a way the apostle would not have done. But these are very much matters of opinion, that can be brought to no very definite test; and therefore the great majority of biblical scholars have thought that, while there is a certain difference in the style of this epistle from those to the Romans, Corinthians, and Galatians, and signs of it having been written later, and in view of different errors, there is nothing to show that it is impossible that

Paul could have written it, or to outweigh the historical testimonies that he did. Many writers on the theology of Paul, or of the New Testament, think proper, for the sake of an absolutely unassailable foundation, to limit their materials to the four great epistles just mentioned; but this does not imply that there is any real or serious reason to doubt that this epistle is his, as it professes to be.

II. TO WHOM ADDRESSED

The epistle has borne from the earliest time, in all known copies, the title "to Ephesians," and has been generally thought by the Church to have been addressed to the Christians in that great commercial city of Asia, where Paul had laboured as an evangelist for three years, and founded an important church. But the title, though as old as the third century, is not a part of the original writing; and there are various strong reasons to think that in this instance it is not quite correct, but that the epistle was addressed to the Christians in the Roman province of Asia who had received the gospel from Ephesus through some of those converted under Paul's ministry there.

1. The first of these reasons is that, in all probability, the words "in Ephesus," which in most of our copies stand in the salutation (ch. i. 1), were not in the original. There is both external and internal evidence against them. External evidence is afforded by the facts (*a*) that they are wanting in the two oldest and best manuscripts, the Vatican and the Sinaitic, both of the fourth century, and (*b*) that Basil, who wrote about the same time, says that in the oldest of the copies in his day the words were absent. Further, (*c*) in the second century, Marcion quoted from this epistle, but called it one to Laodiceans, and Tertullian, his strenuous opponent in the following age, accused him of altering, not the text, but the title of the epistle, and departing from the tradition of the Church; from which it would seem that neither of them read the words in the epistle itself. Thus, the further back we trace the ancient testimony, the more indications do we find of

the absence of these words. That they should have been inserted by copyists, when the epistle universally bore the title "to Ephesians," is more easily explainable than that they should have been omitted, if they were in the original. They are also suspicious on internal grounds, owing to the structure of the sentence. For, if retained, they should in strict grammar be rendered thus: "to the saints who are at Ephesus and faithful." But this is a very awkward combination, in one clause, of a local designation and a description of character; and such a connection is unexampled in Paul's epistles. The very similar salutation in the Epistle to the Colossians is quite different in grammatical construction: "to those at Colossæ, saints and faithful." This confirms the doubt cast on the words by external testimony, and makes it probable that the epistle was not expressly addressed by Paul to the Christians at Ephesus. That it was meant for others besides them, appears also from further reasons.

2. In Col. iv. 16, Paul directs that that epistle be read also in the church of the Laodiceans, and that they also read the epistle from Laodicea. The only natural, if not the only possible, meaning of this is, "the epistle" (which I have sent, and you will get) "from Laodicea." But this cannot have been one addressed exclusively to the Laodiceans; for in that case Paul would have sent his salutations directly to them, instead of bidding the Colossians salute them, as he does (Col. iv. 15). There is great probability that this was the epistle that Paul desired to be read at Colossæ, since it was sent by the hand of Tychicus, a man of Asia, who also bore that to the Colossians: and this would explain how Marcion, who was a native of the neighbouring province of Pontus, came to regard it as addressed to the Laodiceans. If this was not so, we must suppose that an epistle, to which Paul evidently attached importance, has been lost, and also that Paul wrote no fewer than four epistles (to Ephesians, Colossians, Philemon, and Laodiceans), at the same time, to Christians very near to each other. Neither of these suppositions is impossible; but both seem improbable.

3. A third line of argument is drawn from the general character

of the epistle. Paul had preached for three years at Ephesus, and experienced many vicissitudes of remarkable success, and dangerous persecution. He had many intimate and faithful friends in the church there. Yet in this epistle there is not a single reference to his work or trials at Ephesus, nor any mention of a single person there. He speaks of having heard of their faith and love, without the least indication that they had been converted through his own preaching. At one place (iii. 1) his language seems to imply a doubt whether they had heard of his apostolic commission; and though this may not be its only possible construction, any other would make it a sarcastic form of address, occasioned by nothing that we know of, and very unlike Paul. In a word, the epistle bears all the appearance of being addressed to readers with whom, for the most part, the writer was not personally acquainted.

All these various and independent considerations converge towards the conclusion, that the epistle was sent to the Christian communities which had been formed through the apostle's preaching at Ephesus becoming known in the towns and districts round about, extending through a large part of the province of Asia. This opinion, which was suggested by Archbishop Usher, and has been adopted by many modern scholars, is better without the artificial suggestion, that Tychicus was provided with several copies, having blanks left for the insertion of different names. In that case we should expect to find, or to hear of, copies with other names, whereas the oldest copies of which we know had no name at all in the salutation; and its construction is such, that the insertion of the name, and not its absence, presents an anomaly. According to the oldest authorities, the epistle is like that to the Hebrews and the First Epistle of John, which, though bearing no definite address, were intended for a particular set of readers. Tychicus would have instructions to whom he was to deliver it; and since Ephesus was the chief town, and contained the mother church of those addressed, it is not difficult to understand how it came to be endorsed "to Ephesians," when the epistles of Paul were collected into one volume.

In whatever places they lived, the readers addressed were

Gentiles, who had been converted, by the grace of God, from the idolatry and vices of heathenism to faith in the one living and true God and His Son Jesus Christ. The epistle is founded on this fact, and consists largely of an illustration of its greatness and blessedness, and a call to the duties which it involves. They were living in the midst of heathens, from whom they were exposed to temptations to immorality, though not, as far as appears, to anything that could be called persecution. They seem also to have been in danger from the allurements of a certain kind of Christianity that laid more stress on its speculative than on its ethical elements.

III. Time and Circumstances of Writing

Like all the other epistles in the New Testament, this has no formal mention of the place and time at which it was written, and these must be gathered from its contents. But the only definite indication on these points is the statement that, when he sent this letter to Gentile Christians, Paul was "a prisoner of Jesus Christ for their sakes" (iii. 1, 13, iv. 1); that is, that he was in confinement and bonds, because of his work of preaching salvation through Christ to the heathen as well as to God's ancient people of Israel. This exactly describes what is related in Acts, of how the Jews had risen in riot against Paul on his last visit to Jerusalem, and by their violent rage and accusations against him, because of his missionary work among the Gentiles, had caused him to be taken into custody by the Romans, and, after being detained two years at Cæsarea, sent to Rome, where he remained two years longer under military guard, in a hired house, chained to a soldier. So far as the statements in this epistle go, it may have been written at any time during these four years; and some have thought that it should be dated from Cæsarea, in the earlier part of his imprisonment. But it is the more general opinion, and seems much more probable, that it was from Rome that Paul sent this epistle and those to the Colossians and to Philemon. From these it appears that Paul enjoyed some opportunities of preaching the gospel, which corresponds exactly with the situation as described in Acts xxviii. 30, 31 ; whereas in Cæsarea his confinement appears to have been closer. Again, the runaway slave Onesimus, who was converted by Paul in his bonds (Philem. 10), is far more likely to have found his way to Rome than to Cæsarea ; also the companions, from whom he sends greetings to the Colossians, would more probably be with him in Rome. If the Epistle to the Philippians was written before this group, as many scholars think, that would be a conclusive proof, for that epistle shows, by the salutation sent from the saints of Cæsar's household (*i.e.* establishment of slaves), that it was written in Rome. But the relative date of the Epistle to Philippians and the Asian letters is very uncertain ; only in the former Paul is more occupied with the thoughts that fill his earlier epistles, in the latter with some new developments of these. It is not likely that these epistles were written early in Paul's residence in Rome. There had been time for him to hear of the progress and condition of the churches in Macedonia and Asia, and to receive messengers from them ; and there was a good deal to tell them, either by letter or messenger, of his state and work. He also appears to have been expecting a speedy decision of his cause, and probable liberation.

While we can thus ascertain with tolerable accuracy that these epistles were written towards the close of the two years after Paul was brought to Rome, it is not possible to be sure of the exact date of that event. It was in the year after the recall of Felix, and the appointment of Festus to succeed him as procurator of Judæa ; and the year of Felix' recall can only be inferentially determined. It took place in summer, and cannot have been later than 61 A.D. ; while most modern authorities think that it cannot have been more than one or two years earlier, since the rebellion of the Egyptian (Acts xxi. 38) which had happened before Paul's apprehension, can hardly, according to Josephus, have been earlier than 57 A.D. Thus Paul's voyage to Rome might have been either in 59, 60, or 61 ; and the date of the epistle, 62, 63, or 64. But all these calculations depend on the correctness of Josephus' statements, and on one important point, as to the beginning of Felix' government, he is contradicted by Tacitus ; while Eusebius and other ancient writers place the events several years earlier; and they may possibly have based their opinions on older authorities now lost to us. We must therefore remember that our information is too scanty to enable us to be perfectly certain of the date.

It is more important to have a true idea of the state of Christianity at the time.

What now was the condition of Christianity in the world at that time? Besides the original community of believers in Jesus in Jerusalem and Judæa, of which James the Lord's brother was the chief leader, there were churches formed by dispersion and missionary effort from it, in Samaria, Damascus, Antioch, and throughout Syria and Cilicia. The faith was also spreading eastwards; and probably some of the twelve were evangelising in Mesopotamia, and towards the Parthian Empire. Then there were the four great groups of churches founded by Paul, in the provinces of Galatia, Asia, Macedonia, and Achaia; while a large and devoted body of Christians had been formed at Rome. About the same time, the gospel must have been spreading northwards to Pontus, Cappadocia, and Bithynia; and southwards to Egypt, and other parts of Africa. But Paul's missionary labours had been directed by God's guidance ever to the westward, so as to thrust, as it were, a wedge of the new faith and life into the very heart of the heathen Roman Empire. He was ever eagerly looking forward, and from each point that he gained preparing for an advance to a farther one. But, in this eagerness for progress, the apostle of the Gentiles never forgot the necessity of consolidating the conquests already won. He was not a mere evangelist, travelling from place to place: he bore with him, everywhere and every day, the care of all the churches that he had founded; and, just as the Roman Government preserved the unity of its administration by means of letters constantly passing between its different officials, Paul by his epistles kept far-distant churches in touch with him and with one another. Otherwise these churches were isolated indeed. In the great heathen cities they were but single congregations, and the cities and provinces in which they lived were often mutually hostile.

Ephesus and Sardis, Athens and Corinth, were keenly jealous of one another; and between the Galatians, the Macedonians, and the Greeks there was little in common of thought, feeling, or customs. Within single churches there were very apt to be divisions and strifes, between Jews and Gentiles, learned and ignorant, rich and poor, which Paul had often cause to reprove. But the apostle's aim was that they should be at one, not only among themselves, but with all the household of faith; and to that purpose he applied both deep thought and careful effort.

In what way he did so, may be best seen from the fifteenth chapter of his Epistle to the Romans, the last which he wrote before his imprisonment, in which he takes a survey of his past work, and indicates his plans and purposes for the future. He recalls how he has preached the gospel from Jerusalem round about to Illyricum, taking as his fields of labour regions where Christ had not yet been known. He looks still farther to the west, and desires to make a journey into Spain, and his intended visit to Rome is only a step towards that further evangelisation. But, before he undertakes it, he looks once more towards the east, and is going up to Jerusalem. What was the object of this? It was to minister to the saints there, the original Christian community. The churches of Macedonia and Achaia, and, as appears also, those of Galatia and Asia, *i.e.* all the groups of Gentile churches founded by Paul, had, at his suggestion and encouragement, made a collection, to supply the poverty of the mother church; and he was going to convey it to Jerusalem. But why should Paul delay his long-desired westward journey by taking these gifts up in person? There were many trustworthy companions and assistants to whom this duty might be assigned. It must have been because more was involved than the mere safe and faithful transmission of pecuniary gifts. It was intended to be an expression of brotherly goodwill on the part of the Gentile believers to the Jews, giving them a recognition, by material things, for the spiritual blessings of which they had been made partakers; and it was to be conveyed to them by a number of chosen representatives from each of the groups of churches concerned. The object was to show the unity, in love and mutual interest, of the churches in the heathen world with that of Israel, and, if possible, to remove any jealousy or enmity between them. Hence it had a certain sacred and solemn character: it was a sort of sacrificial offering of the Gentile churches themselves to the God of Israel (Rom. xv. 16), and was to be brought at one of the great annual feasts, that of Pentecost, at which the Spirit had been sent down, and the Church of Christ formally inaugurated. This explains why Paul thought it necessary to go up himself, and why he expresses so much anxiety that his ministration might be acceptable to the saints in Jerusalem. It was the practical means by which he sought to bind together the churches of the Gentiles and of Israel.

But the result had not answered Paul's hopes. The gifts had been received; but the apostle personally had been met with doubts and scruples, and when he was assailed by the Jewish mob, and taken into custody by the Romans, there is no record of any effort on the part of the Jerusalem church to save or to encourage him. Now he is at Rome as a prisoner, whither he had desired to come as a free messenger of Christ; but he has the hope of liberation being possible and near at hand. If he is to resume his missionary activity, would he not do so in the same spirit of courage and wisdom, looking forward to fresh fields, and yet not forgetting those won before, and still aiming at the unity of the Christian churches, though not exactly by the same means as before? He has heard of new and dangerous opinions in the church at Colossæ, in regard to which he sends them an epistle, and he proposes, if released, to visit them; for still, as before, he will not prosecute further enterprises without first consolidating former conquests. And as he is concerned not only for the healthful growth of each several church, but for their union and harmony as one whole, he writes this general epistle to the churches in Asia, more especially to enforce those catholic and peace-loving thoughts that had before found tangible expression in the collection for the saints at Jerusalem. Although there was much to cause him anxiety in the state of the Christian communities among the Gentiles, yet he saw, with gratitude and praise to God, that they were really thriving, and that in them was realised the idea of a people of God, in which all national distinctions were abolished, and Jew and Greek, barbarians, Scythian, bond and free, were all brothers in Christ. The one Church of God in all the world, as the counterpart of the Israel of God, had arisen as a reality out of the gospel that he preached; and it would almost seem as if the result had surpassed his expectation. Hence the joyful and exultant tone of this epistle, very wonderful in view of the fettered and helpless condition of the writer, and the opposition to which his teaching was still exposed. He has heard news of the gospel bearing fruit everywhere, in all the world (see Col. i. 5); and so amid all his sufferings and anxieties he is cheered, and he recognises God's hand thus carrying out an eternal purpose. In these circumstances, such a letter as this is not unnatural.

IV. Scope and Contents of the Letter

It begins with an expression of fervent praise to God for the wonderful blessings He has bestowed on him and his readers, in Christ, and the way in which He is disclosing in actual reality His eternal purpose of gathering into one all things in Christ (i. 3–14). From this Paul passes to a prayer for those to whom he writes, that they may know, by the teaching of the Spirit of God, the full blessedness of their position, and the greatness of what God has done, and is doing, in and for them (i. 15–ii. 10). Next, he reminds them especially how they, who were Gentile strangers, have been incorporated in the household of God (ii. 11–22); and then comes a special appeal to them, on the ground of his position as the prisoner of Christ for them (iii. 1), which is interrupted by a digression to explain this (iii. 2–13). These sections, with the prayer that follows (iii. 15–23), are often regarded as forming a first or doctrinal part of the epistle, followed by a second or practical part of equal length (iv., v., vi.), containing exhortations to the course of conduct becoming their position. But this way of dividing the epistle is too formal, and does not correspond to its real course of thought. The contents of the first three chapters are not an exposition of doctrine, like the earlier part of the Epistle to the Romans, nor a warning against error, such as we find in those to the Galatians and Colossians; they are rather the outpouring of the apostle's thankfulness and affectionate interest in the Asian churches. These lead him to prolong the preliminary part of his letter, and it is only at ch. iii. 1 that he comes to what is his proper object in writing it. For reasons indicated in the following exposition, I think the translators of the Authorised Version were right in extending the digression to the end of ch. iii., so that ch. iv. resumes and carries on the address in ch. iii. 1. From this it appears that the special object of Paul in this epistle was to give the moral precepts contained in chs. iv.–vi., the divisions and connections of which are indicated in the notes. He was on the point of entering on them after the first two chapters, and indeed had them in view from the very beginning. In his view, what the churches needed, beside and even above the warning against doctrinal error which he gave in his letter to the Colossians, was the keeping before them of the high standard of Christian morality, according to the teaching of Jesus Himself, and founded on their experience of salvation in Him.

In fact, Paul never was anxious about correct belief simply as such; he was jealous for the gospel, not as a system of truth, but as the glad tidings of God's mercy in Christ to all men, even the vilest sinners; and he was stern and vehement against any teaching that denied that: he believed, too, that this gospel was the best and only way of securing real purity of heart and life; and he was equally severe against all who, believing in God's grace, were careless of holy living. His battle against legalism in its open form had been fought and won; and now his zeal is for Christian morality. The danger from incipient Gnostic speculations was, in his eyes, not so much that they were false in doctrine, as that they perverted spiritual morality; hence he set up, as a positive defence against them, the profound exhibition of Christian ethics contained in this epistle. The later church teachers, from Irenæus onwards, who had to deal with full-blown Gnosticism, met it as a speculation by formulating Christianity in the Creeds; but they allowed the subtle influence of its ascetic dualism to corrupt the morals of Christendom, and ultimately to pervert the gospel into the superstitious and unhealthy system of the mediæval Church. Paul had shown a more excellent way, and, had the spirit of his teaching been retained, that degeneracy might have been avoided; while the preservation of his teaching, and of that of Jesus Himself, made a Reformation of the Church possible, when they were again understood and applied.

V. Relation of the Epistle to other parts of the New Testament

It is interesting and useful for the understanding of this epistle, to observe how it is related to other New Testament writings, both earlier and later. When it was written, there were in existence Paul's earlier epistles to the Thessalonians, Galatians, Corinthians, and Romans, and possibly also the Epistle of James, though its date cannot be determined, and is thought by many to have been some years later. Oral accounts of the teaching and life of Jesus were current, and probably also some of the attempts at written records, to which Luke refers (Luke i. 1); but it is not likely that any of the Gospels as we have them were composed; and all the other books of the New Testament were certainly later. The epistle is most nearly related to (1) that to the Colossians, which was despatched by the same messenger. The relation of these is that of two letters by the same author at the same time, and partly about the same subjects. Hence they run more nearly parallel than any other epistles of Paul, for no others were sent by him together, and most of them were separated by pretty long intervals. The short letter to Philemon was also written at the same time, and throws light upon Paul's circumstances and position in regard to the social relations of the age.

(2) During the same imprisonment, but some time earlier or later, was written the Epistle to the Philippians. It contains more of Paul's personal feelings and experiences, but is similar to this and to that to

the Colossians, in having for its main object the inculcation of practical morality, and in its lofty teaching about the glory of Christ and the relation of His person and work to the whole universe.

A connection may also be traced (3) between this and the earlier epistles of Paul, through that part of his letter to the Romans in which he explains the principles and plans of his missionary work (Rom. xv.). For there he shows how it was the will of God that Gentiles and Jews should form one body, and how his missionary movements and designs were directed towards the practical realisation of that great end. The thoughts expanded in this epistle are just the filling in of the outline there sketched, showing how, in accordance with God's purpose, His kingdom was to include not only His ancient people Israel, but all who were being gathered from among the heathen nations by faith in Christ to the fellowship of the children of God. This thought again arose from the great truths unfolded in the earlier part of the Epistle to the Romans, of the universal need of the gospel as a revelation of God's righteousness and salvation to all alike, to the Jew first, and also to the Gentile. Thus the letter to the Ephesians and other Christians in Asia, is a natural development, and crowning fruit, of the main teaching of Paul through all his ministry.

But our epistle has a further relation (4) to the First Epistle of Peter. That is addressed to the Christians in the province of Asia, along with those in the neighbouring ones of Pontus, Galatia, Cappadocia, and Bithynia; and it bears evident traces of the acquaintance of its writer with this one. The general scheme of thought is the same, that of believers in Jesus being the true Israel, the new people of God, whom He has chosen and redeemed; and the great aim is the same, to enforce the necessity of a truly Christian life. Many of the more particular thoughts are the same, such as the election of God, the redemption and example of Christ, the mutual duties of various relations. Yet, both in the epistle as a whole, and in its particular parts, there are characteristic differences, showing that the one is not a servile copy of the other; and that, if Peter was indebted to Paul for some of his ideas, he was quite independent and original in his way of working them out. What Paul expresses in transcendent and mystical generalisations, the apostle of the circumcision presents in concrete historical pictures; and thus, even when the theme is the same, we cannot help seeing that the truth has been assimilated by two different minds, and expressed by each in the way natural to himself, so that we cannot mistake the one for the other. The First Epistle of Peter stands in some respects in a similar relation also to that of James, and Second Peter to that of Jude. The date of the First Epistle of Peter is uncertain, but it was probably after the outbreak of Nero's persecution of the Christians, while Paul's Asian and Philippian epistles were before that event.

(5) Paul's Epistles to Timothy are connected with this one; because they refer to the state of the Christians in and about Ephesus some years later, and exhibit the apostle's anxiety in reference to views similar to those controverted in the Epistle to the Colossians, and also his supreme concern for godliness and purity of life. If he does not rise in them to the lofty and wide-reaching views of his earlier letters, but deals more with details and personal directions to his son Timothy, he keeps before him the same great aims, and has in view similar circumstances and dangers.

(6) In the Apocalypse (ii., iii.), we learn something of the spiritual condition of the churches in Asia at a later period, when the Neronian persecution had certainly begun, and extended its rage to this province, where there had already been confessors and martyrs for the cause of Christ. One important coincidence between the Apocalypse and this epistle is in the conception of the Church as the Bride, the Lamb's wife (Rev. xxi. 9). The warnings against those who falsely call themselves apostles (Rev. ii. 2), and who say they are Jews and are not (Rev. ii. 9, iii. 9), are not, as some critics think, directed against Paul; for they are just parallel to his own words (2 Cor. xi. 13), and his claim for Christians to be the true circumcision, against the legal Jews, whom he calls the concision (Phil. iii. 2, 3).

Finally, (7) a careful study of this epistle leaves on my mind no doubt that Paul was acquainted with, and referred to, the teaching of our Lord. There is, indeed, no express reference to His authority, such as is made on certain points in 1 Corinthians; but the moral exhortations which begin at Eph. iv. 20 are so coloured with the ideas contained in the Evangelists' records of Jesus' teaching, including some in the Fourth Gospel, and this section is introduced by so distinct a reference to the truth as it is in Jesus, the historic Saviour, that it seems impossible to deny that the apostle was enforcing what he knew to be the precepts of his Master. He does not, however, repeat them so literally as is done, for example, in the "Teaching of the Twelve Apostles": he gives them as they had passed through his mind and heart, but he preserves the spirit of them much better than that early Christian text-book.

Luke was with Paul when he sent this and its companion letters, and very possibly he had already written his Gospel; if not, he must have collected the materials; and in all likelihood the collection of discourses of the Lord in Hebrew by Matthew had also been written; while during Paul's two years' detention in Cæsarea he might easily have heard reports of Jesus' discourses contained in the Fourth Gospel, though the composition of that Gospel itself is generally thought to have been many years later. In one place in this epistle (iv. 13), the thought seems to have been derived from a discourse of Christ in John (iii. 20, 21), and is much clearer when read in connection with it. (See note on the passage.)

There is also reason to believe that Paul was acquainted with some sayings of our Lord that have not been included in the canonical Gospels. One such is expressly quoted in the speech reported by Luke as addressed to the elders of the Ephesian church (Acts xx. 35), "to remember the words of the Lord Jesus, how He said, It is more blessed to give than to receive." From the source from which he learned this, Paul may have derived other words of Christ; and scholars have of late been searching with great care all the remains of early Christian literature, to see what traces can be found of sayings of Jesus not recorded in the Gospels. These have been called *Agrapha*, *i.e.* unwritten by the Evangelists.

Recent discoveries of early Christian writings that had been long lost, such as the "Teaching of the Twelve," and the close of what is called the Second Epistle of Clement, have added to the materials, and to the means of testing by comparison such sayings; and references to words of Christ have been detected in places of the epistles where they were not suspected before.

This inquiry is of great interest and importance. It has proved that there were in circulation reports of Jesus' teaching, and these probably in writing, considerably earlier than the time to which any of our Gospels can be traced, and thus we have an additional guarantee that the evangelic picture of Jesus is truly historical. And it also shows that the teaching of Christ and of the apostles forms one whole; that their theology was founded upon His revelation; and that it is unreasonable to reject the doctrine of the disciples if we accept that of the Master.

A large collection of sayings ascribed to Jesus, but not found in our Gospels, has been made by Alfred Resch, and he detects allusions in the Epistle to the Ephesians to a larger number of these than in any other of Paul's epistles. Though his collection needs sifting, it may be of some use to mention these here.

(a) Macarius, near the end of the fourth century, writes: "The Lord said to them, Why marvel ye at the signs? I give you a great inheritance which the whole world has not." And Resch thinks that this is a genuine saying of Christ, because of the general trustworthiness of the writer, of its resemblance in style to those in the Synoptic Gospels, and of Pauline parallels, especially in Eph. i. 17, 18.

(b) In the very ancient homily known as the Second Epistle of Clement, we read: "The Lord Himself, when once asked by some one when His kingdom shall come, said, When the two shall be one, and the inside as the outside, and the male with the female, neither male nor female." To this Resch thinks there are parallels in Eph. ii. 14, 16, "He hath made them both one;" v. 22, 32, Christ with the Church as the husband with the wife; and Gal. iii. 28, "neither male nor female."

(*c*) The editor of the Apostolic Constitutions, immediately after citing Christ's words in Matt. x. 12, adds : "As it is written 'to them that are near and to them that are far off, whom the Lord knew as being His.'" This is parallel to Eph. ii. 17 and 2 Tim. ii. 19, and is thought to point to a saying of Jesus in which both were combined.

(*d*) Clement of Alexandria writes : "For, saith the Lord, they who do the will of My Father are My brethren and fellow-heirs : call not therefore to you a father on earth, for there are masters on earth, but in heaven the Father, of whom is all fatherhood in heaven and on earth." Here the peculiar words of Eph. iii. 15 are expressly quoted as part of a saying of the Lord.

(*e*) The words in Eph. iv. 26, "Let not the sun go down upon your wrath," were quoted by more than one ancient writer as spoken by the Lord, and as being in the Gospel, though by others they are referred simply to the Scripture.

(*f*) In the Clementine Homilies (xix. 2), Peter is made to say, "And elsewhere He said, He that sowed the bad seed is the devil ; and again, Give no pretext to the evil one ;" which is parallel to Eph. iv. 27.

(*g*) In the Teaching of the Twelve, among a series of sayings of Christ, this occurs (i. 6) : "But concerning this also it hath been said, Let thine alms sweat into thine hands till thou know to whom thou givest." Resch compares with this Eph. iv. 28.

(*h*) In an ancient tract, wrongly ascribed to Cyprian (*de aleatoribus*, iii.), this is found : "The Lord warns us and says, Grieve not the Holy Spirit who is in you, and quench not the light which has shined in you," a close parallel to Eph. iv. 30.

(*i*) The saying in Eph. v. 14 ("Wherefore he saith, Awake thou that sleepest," etc.) is said by some of the Fathers to have been taken from the Apocalypse of Elias, which they regarded as genuine, but is now known to have been a late forgery, but to have contained some sayings of Christ from a written collection earlier than our Gospels. Hence Resch infers that Paul took it directly from this collection, and that he quotes it as a saying of Christ.

When we examine these instances, for the purpose of throwing light on the epistle, it must be acknowledged that (*a*) and (*b*), even if they do probably point to real sayings of Christ, have only very general or partial resemblances to the parallels cited from the epistle, so that there is very slight reason to think that Paul was acquainted with them. In (*c*) the apostle's words have so sufficient an explanation in Old Testament language, that there seems but little ground for tracing them to a saying of Christ. It is otherwise with (*d*); and I am inclined to agree with Resch in regard to it. In considering (*e*), we cannot ignore the possibility that those who had the whole New Testament in their hands may have ascribed the precept to Christ, either by a lapse of memory, or as believing that the Lord spoke through the apostle. The instances (*f*) and (*h*) seem very probably real, but (*g*) has a very slight resemblance to Paul's words, so that, whatever the probability of its being a genuine saying of Christ, there seems none at all for the supposition that the apostle had it in his mind. As to (*i*), the decision is very difficult, but perhaps, on the whole, Resch's facts and arguments make it probable that the quotation is from a saying of Jesus.

In the following notes the Revised Version is used, as being more exact than the Authorised, which is printed above; and where the difference is important, the reasons for it are explained.

PAUL'S EPISTLE TO THE EPHESIANS

I. 1, 2. *The Salutation.*—Paul begins this, like all his epistles, in the customary form, mentioning his own name and those whom he addresses, with a good wish, in which the ordinary form of greeting is elevated to a Christian prayer.

CHAP. I. 1. PAUL, an apostle of Jesus Christ by the will of God, to the saints which are at Ephesus, and 2 to the faithful in Christ Jesus: grace *be* to you, and peace,

1. **Paul,**] Here, as in the Epistle to the Romans, he does not associate any of his companions with himself, as he does in all his other public letters; the reason possibly being that, like that epistle, this one is very general in its subject, and intended partly for those with whom he was not personally acquainted.

an apostle of Christ Jesus]—*i.e.* a missionary or envoy sent by the Messiah Jesus. The name Christ, however, is often used by Paul merely as a proper name, though he is quite conscious of its original meaning, the anointed—*i.e.* the Saviour and King whom God had promised and sent—and sometimes uses it in that sense (as in v. 10, 12). He declares himself to have been sent and commissioned by Jesus as a messenger, and further on he explains what was the meaning and purpose of the message with which he was entrusted.

through the will of God,] This clause is added, as also in 1 and 2 Corinthians, Colossians, and 2 Timothy, to show that his mission had divine authority. In writing to those by whom his apostleship was not called in question, Paul prefers to style himself simply a bondsman of Christ (so in 1 and 2 Thessalonians, Philippians, and Philemon); in addressing the Galatians and Romans, he dilates with more fulness on the source and purpose of his apostleship; here, and in writing to the Corinthians and Colossians, he uses an intermediate form.

to the saints (or holy) who are also faithful (or believers) in Christ Jesus:] As shown in the Introduction, this is most probably the original form of the clause, and it describes not two classes of people, but only one, who are marked by two characteristic qualities, holiness and faith.

from God our Father, and *from* the Lord Jesus Christ.

The idea conveyed by the first word, which, like the second, is an adjective, is not piety or moral purity, but separation from the world to God, not merely, however, in an outward or ceremonial sense, as the Jews were separated from other nations by peculiar forms of ritual and worship, but in a truly religious sense. It may be explained by what Paul says of the Thessalonians, that they "turned to God from idols to serve the living and true God" (1 Thess. i. 9).

They are described as being also faithful. The word thus rendered generally means, in classical Greek, "trustworthy," but in the New Testament it sometimes undoubtedly has the sense of believing (see John xx. 27; Gal. iii. 9), and in all probability that is its meaning here, as in Col. i. 2; 1 Pet. i. 21.

"In Christ Jesus" may be taken either as expressing the object of their faith, or as standing by itself to denote that intimate spiritual relation of union to Christ of which Paul speaks so much, and very specially in this epistle. This latter construction is thought by some to be grammatically necessary; but that can hardly be made out, and the other one seems to be more natural. Still the expression is an emphatic one, bringing out the closeness and intimacy of the connection between faith and its object, not merely believing about Christ, or upon Christ, but in Christ, so as to be spiritually united to Him. The whole description may be illustrated by what Paul declares in Acts xx. 21 to have been the substance of his teaching at Ephesus, "repentance toward God, and faith toward our Lord Jesus."

This address describes the character of those who are truly Christians; and yet the letter was undoubtedly intended for all the members of the church or churches to which Tychicus was instructed to deliver it. Paul did not mean to assure all these that they were certainly holy and believers in Christ; for in the course of the epistle (iv. 21), he hints that possibly this may not be so. We are not, however, on that account to lower the meaning of the words he uses here, as if they meant a merely external holiness and faith, or were simply a charitable form of salutation. They are grounded on the fact that all members of the Christian Church profess to be separated from the world to God, and trusting in Christ Jesus. Unless their profession is false, they really are so; and it is right and fitting that they should be addressed on the assumption that their profession is true. When the real meaning and implications of that profession are explained as faithfully as they are by Paul, this is the best way to detect and awaken hypocrites and self-deceivers.

2. Grace to you and peace from God our Father and the Lord Jesus Christ.] This is Paul's usual salutation, in which he Christianises the customary form by putting, instead of "greeting," the kindred word "grace," and adds to it the Hebrew expression " peace," mentioning as the source of both, God our Father and the Lord Jesus Christ. The Greeks were wont to wish their friends joy: Paul wishes his brethren the favour of God, which gives the truest joy; and as a Hebrew he joins with that peace as the abiding sum of all real good. Both he invokes alike from God our Father and the Lord Jesus Christ, thus implying that the divine favour, and the inward peace that accompanies it, come as truly from Jesus Christ as from God the Father. Both alike grant divine favour, and both have access to the secret soul of man to give peace there. This habitual association of our Lord with God

3 Blessed *be* the God and Father of our Lord Jesus Christ, who hath blessed us with all spiritual blessings in heavenly

the Father, as giving the highest and most inward blessings, is a very strong proof that Paul believed the true deity of Christ.

I. 3-14. *Praise for Salvation.*—How real this salutation was, and how deeply Paul felt the wonder and the happiness involved in the fact that he could address people in a distant province as holy and believers in Christ, and confidently pray for God's grace and peace to them, appears from this, that immediately after he breaks out into a rapturous expression of blessing and praise to God. With a similar doxology, beginning with the very same words, he opened his Second Epistle to the Corinthians; but there it was his personal gratitude, for escape from danger and relief from painful anxieties, that prompted the utterance (2 Cor. i. 3-11). Here no such special reference appears: it is the blessings of Christianity in general that are the theme of praise to God. Writing to many to whom he has no other tie than that of a God-sent missionary of Christ to those who are the people of God through faith in Christ, and thinking of that relation, which was a new thing in the world then, he cannot but praise God, whose eternal purpose of love has brought it about. The whole paragraph (vers. 3-14) is an unfolding, in the form of praise to God, of what is implied in the designation of those to whom he wrote as holy and believers in Christ Jesus.

It is one long and involved sentence, in which, by reason of the fulness of thought, one clause leads on to another, connected by participles and relatives, until the divine grace has been traced from its origin in eternity to our experience of it here and now. It has been likened to a skilfully wrought chain, whose links are so curiously interlaced, that it is not easy to tell where one ends and another begins.

3. **Blessed be the God and Father of our Lord Jesus Christ,**] God is praised under His full New Testament title, which indicates His twofold relation to Christ and to us in Him. He is His God, as incarnate, having become truly man, and therefore sharing our relation to His Father, especially as He bore our sins on the cross (Matt. xxvii. 46; Mark xv. 34). But at the same time God is His Father, as He is the eternal Word, God only begotten (John i. 18), and He makes us partakers of this relation to God, as He said after His resurrection, "I ascend unto my Father, and your Father; my God, and your God" (John xx. 17). In this relation to Christ we bless God, and He has blessed us. Blessing is, literally, speaking well: our blessing of God can only be gratefully declaring His greatness and goodness; but since He speaks and it is done, when He blesses, He makes holy and happy.

who hath blessed us with every spiritual blessing in the heavenly places in Christ,] As we love because He first loved us, so we bless Him who first blessed us, and did so in the very highest way; as Paul shows by stating (1) the nature, (2) the place, and (3) the Mediator of the blessings.

(1) As to its nature, it is "every spiritual blessing." This has been differently explained, as meaning, either benefiting the spirit of man, or bestowed by the Spirit of God; but in effect both come to the same thing. There are good things which we have in common with all animals, such as life, health, vigour, pleasurable sensations: these may be called physical blessings: there are those which we have in common with our fellow-men, whether they are godly or not, such as knowledge, art, taste, society, which

may be called mental blessings; but those which we have in common with the saints and believers in Christ, such as peace of conscience, renewal of heart, assurance of God's love, joy in God, and hope of His glory, are spiritual blessings, as belonging to that part of our nature in which we have contact with God, who is Spirit. Such blessings Paul richly enjoyed, even though in his labours and sufferings for Christ he had little of physical or social enjoyment.

(2) As to its place, this blessing is "in the heavenlies": for so the phrase is literally, though the word *places*, supplied by our translators, gives the meaning correctly. The phrase occurs four times in this epistle, and nowhere else in Scripture. It does not, however, seem to denote anything different from the common expression "in heaven": and Paul may have chosen the unusual form, because he was employing it in an ideal sense. For he does not mean to say here, that God who blesses us is in heaven; that would be a useless truism; and the position of the clause in the sentence shows that it refers to us. We who are blessed are in the heavenlies. How that is so appears from what is said in ver. 20, that God has made Christ to sit at His right hand in the heavenly places; and in ch. ii. 6, that he has raised us up with Him, and made us to sit with Him in the heavenly places. What more particularly is meant by this will be learned when we come to the exposition of these passages: meanwhile the general sense is indicated by the following words, in which (3) the Mediator of the blessing is mentioned, "in Christ." This denotes something more than merely "through Christ," or "for his sake." It implies that He is not only the messenger who brings God's blessing to us, or even the Redeemer who has merited it on our behalf: He is the head or representative, with whom we must be united, if we would receive it. We are in Him, as the branches are in the vine; and the blessing comes to us only because it is first bestowed on Christ our head, like the precious ointment on the head of Aaron, that flowed down his beard, and went to the skirts of his garments. This idea, of believers being in Christ, runs through the whole of this epistle, and may be said to be its keynote; the various aspects and relations of it will appear from the different statements and illustrations given in following passages: here it is simply mentioned in general, as the way in which every spiritual blessing is ours.

By "us" in this place Paul clearly means, in the first instance, himself and those to whom he writes; but since he addresses them in no other character than as saints and believers in Christ, what he says of them holds good also of all those who have truly turned from sin and the world to God, and are trusting in Jesus Christ; but of them only. Paul has made no mention as yet of the collective body of believers as constituting the Church, of which he has afterwards so much to say in this epistle: and the blessings for which he blesses God are surely such as men receive and enjoy personally; hence we cannot regard him as speaking here only of a collective body in general, without having in view the individuals of which it is composed.

When Paul speaks of God blessing us in Christ, he probably has in his mind the promise God made to Abraham (Gen. xxii. 18), "In thy seed shall all the nations of the earth be blessed;" and indicates of what seed that promise is to be understood, as he declares more explicitly in Gal. iii. 7-29. The whole clause is constructed in the spirit of the O. T. revelation, and declares its N. T. fulfilment.

In what follows down to ver. 14 he illustrates the greatness and preciousness of the blessing. First, he refers to the eternal purpose according to which it

4 *places* in Christ: according as he hath chosen us in him before the foundation of the world, that we should be holy 5 and without blame before him in love: having predestinated

is bestowed (vers. 4–6*a*). This shows that our blessing is not merely a recent thing, or, as it were, a second thought of God, but had been determined from the beginning, and is therefore sure (Chrysostom).

4. **even as he chose us in him before the foundation of the world,**] This also is an Old Testament expression, used of Israel (Deut. xiv. 2): "Thou art an holy people unto the LORD thy God, and the LORD hath chosen thee to be a peculiar people unto himself, above (or out of) all peoples that are upon the face of the earth;" also Ps. cxxxv. 4; Isa. xli. 8, 9, xlii. 1. The form of the word rendered "chose" indicates a taking out for Himself; and the passage just quoted suggests that it is out of all peoples of the earth, or, as Jesus says, "I chose you out of the world" (John xv. 19). There, indeed, the word probably refers to the act of Jesus selecting and calling His disciples; but here, since it is expressly said to have been done " before the foundation of the world," it must denote the eternal purpose of God. Even in its historical use, the selection is an act of the mind determining to take some out of a mass, which must be conceived as preceding the call by which they are actually taken; and Paul here declares that God's act in blessing us is performed in accordance with a choice that preceded our existence and that of the whole world. This idea is in harmony with the whole strain of Bible teaching, which represents God as knowing the end from the beginning, and having a purpose which He carries out by means of all things that take place. This is connected with the election of His people in Ps. xxxiii. 11, 12. This choice is said to be " in Christ," and these words refer, as in ver. 3, not to God, but to us. Not, God in Christ chose us; but, God chose us in Christ. As the actual blessings are bestowed on us in Christ, *i.e.* on Christ first and on us as united to Christ; so the choice, before the world was, is of Christ as the head, and of us as members of His body. Christ the God-man is primarily God's elect or chosen One (Isa. xlii. 1–7; Matt. xii. 18–21); but as the Servant of the Lord in the prophecy is sometimes the people, and sometimes He who is "the covenant of the people," so the election of Christ involves that of those who are to be holy and believing in Him.

that we should be holy and without blemish before him,] Although some excellent expositors understand this as referring to our acceptance before God as righteous for Christ's sake, it is more natural to take it as describing personal character. It goes, indeed, far beyond what is attained in this life; but perfect separation to God and freedom from all moral blemish even in the eyes of God, who knows all things and searches the heart, is the ultimate state to which believers have been eternally chosen by God. Our election is not merely to salvation, or to privilege, but to holiness and moral perfection, and that involves duty and service.

in love:] It is a question whether these words are to be connected with what goes before, or with what follows. The oldest MSS. have no punctuation, and therefore cannot determine; and of the two earliest translations, the Latin connects them with the preceding, while the Syriac, along with the most ancient Greek expositors, connects them with what follows. Either construction gives a true and good sense; and the decision must turn on which it is most likely Paul meant, in view of his general usage of language. If the words belong to ver. 4, they might be construed with "he chose us";

us unto the adoption of children by Jesus Christ to himself,
6 according to the good pleasure of his will, to the praise of the
glory of his grace, wherein he hath made us accepted in the

but that is so far separated by intervening clauses, that it is more probable that they qualify "holy and without blemish," and describe love as the sum of moral perfection. But it has been observed that in ch. v. 27 and Col. ii. 22, both parallel passages, and the only other places where the phrase "holy and without blemish" occurs in N. T., it has no such qualifying addition; and it is perhaps more emphatic, standing alone in bare simplicity. On the other side it has been urged, that in all the other clauses of this paragraph the verb is put first, as is natural, since it is the acts of God that are most prominent in the apostle's mind. On the whole, however, the balance of probability seems to be in favour of the connection with ver. 5. Thus taken, the words express the love of God, which is the ground of His eternal election and predestination.

5. having foreordained us unto adoption as sons through Jesus Christ unto himself,] This clause further explains the eternal choice just asserted, and brings to view another aspect of it. Foreordained is the word that represents the more technical term "predestinated," and it means appointed beforehand to a certain end. The prefix "*fore*" has relation to the time when the appointment actually takes effect; and since the verbs are so connected, that the act denoted by this must be either previous to, or at least contemporaneous with that expressed by the former, the foreordination, like the election, must be before the foundation of the world. Both are eternal, and if there be any relation of priority between them, it can only be in nature, not in time; and even so, only in our imperfect manner of conceiving the transcendent thoughts of God. But the difference of the two terms would seem to be, that election refers specially to the persons chosen; foreordination to the end appointed for them.

That is here declared to be adoption as sons, being put by God's appointment into the relation of sons to God. Similarly in Rom. viii. 29, he had said, "Whom he foreknew, he also foreordained to be conformed to the image of his Son, that he might be the firstborn among many brethren." Here this foreordination to adoption is said to be through Jesus Christ, of whom God had been called the Father (ver. 3). By His mediation we are made sons of God, as Paul had explained in his epistle to the Galatians (iii. 26–iv. 7).

according to the good pleasure of his will,] This states the primary cause to which all this purpose, and choice, and blessing are to be traced. It is nothing else than the free and gracious will of God. The word rendered "good pleasure" has two meanings in Scripture. Sometimes it denotes simply the sovereignty of God, in virtue of which He does what seems good in His sight, without needing to give account of any of His matters. So Jesus uses the verb in Matt. xi. 26; Luke x. 21. But since God's sovereignty is always exercised in kindness and grace towards His creatures, the word has also the meaning of good will, benevolence; and as this sense is more common in Paul's writings, I am disposed to understand it so here. But even though the apostle does not emphasise the sovereignty of God's purpose, it is to be observed that he traces it back to His will, not to any necessity of His nature or character.

6. to the praise of the glory of his grace,] The end answers to the

7 beloved. In whom we have redemption through his blood, the forgiveness of sins, according to the riches of his grace: beginning of this divine plan. As its cause is sovereign good will, its final purpose is that God's grace be known and praised. God's grace is His free, self-moving love, bestowing good without money or price upon the needy and unworthy. That grace has glory essentially belonging to it, for it is Godlike; it shows in the highest degree the absolute perfection, the infinite moral greatness and goodness of God. The praise of this glory is an end altogether worthy of God, because it implies the greatest holiness and happiness of His creatures, by whom He is thus known, loved, and enjoyed as the Supreme Good.

which he freely bestowed on us (*or* wherewith he endued us) in the Beloved:] The word which is thus variously rendered is a very rare one, and the construction is peculiar. It is a verb formed from the noun *grace*, so that it would be literally, "with which he graced us;" and since grace, here and elsewhere in N. T., means free favour, the meaning seems to be, He showed us favour. So, in the only other place where the word occurs in N. T., it is rightly rendered, "thou that art highly favoured" (Luke i. 28). The notion that it means "filled with graciousness," adopts a meaning of "grace" that became common in the Church in later times, but does not appear in N. T. God's favour, like all spiritual blessings, is bestowed on us in Christ, who is here called, very emphatically, "the Beloved." To us God's good will shows itself as grace, bestowing blessings on poor, weak, and guilty creatures; to Him in whom we receive it, who is the eternal Son of God, it goes forth simply as love. Grace, mercy, pity, compassion, long-suffering, are all included in love, and are the rainbow hues into which the white light that shines in heaven is refracted, as it passes through the clouds of sins and sorrows that envelop our earth.

7. **in whom we have our redemption through his blood, the forgiveness of our trespasses, according to the riches of his grace,**] Here first Paul uses the present tense, "we have," in this doxology. He has passed from the consideration of the eternal purpose of God to bless us, which shows so marvellously the depth and greatness of His love; and he now proceeds to contemplate the actual accomplishment of that purpose, in the work of Christ for us, and the work of the Holy Spirit in us. The line of thought, that began with "even as" (ver. 4), has now been brought to a close; and this verse might as well be connected with ver. 3, as with the immediately preceding, to which it is grammatically attached.

Redemption is literally buying out, or ransoming, *i.e.* procuring deliverance by the payment of a price. But it is not seldom used in a general sense, for a deliverance that is as sure as if a price had been paid. Here, however, there is reason to believe that Paul used it in its proper sense. For he mentions the means of deliverance, "through his blood," *i.e.* His death on the cross, which elsewhere in this epistle (ch. v. 2, 25) he views as a giving Himself up for us. Since, in Gal. iii. 13, he had said, "Christ bought us out from the curse of the law, becoming a curse for us;" and in Rom. iii. 24-26 he had spoken, as here, of redemption in Christ through His blood, and explained that this was that God might be just in justifying believers; we cannot doubt that Paul meant here, that Christ's death was the ransom given to the law and justice of God for our deliverance. This doctrine is founded on the words of Jesus Himself, who declared that He came to give His life a ransom

8 wherein he hath abounded toward us in all wisdom and

for many, that He laid it down at His Father's command, and that His blood was that of the new covenant shed for the remission of sins.

Here, too, our redemption is identified with the remission (*i.e.* forgiveness) of our trespasses, which shows that the evil or bondage from which we are redeemed is here viewed as the guilt of sin, or the condemnation which God's law and justice pronounce against it, which is taken away by remission. No doubt redemption has, in Paul's view, many other aspects; it is "from all iniquity" (Tit. ii. 14), "from this present evil world" (Gal. i. 4), and there is an ultimate "redemption of the body" for which we wait (Rom. viii. 23). What we have in Christ is a redemption from every kind of bondage; and there is no real deliverance from evil of any kind, except through the blood of Christ. But that which in Paul's view is the beginning and condition of all the rest, is deliverance from the bondage of guilt, by the remission of our trespasses.

This is done "according to the riches of God's grace." Paul has no fear that redemption through Christ's blood might obscure the grace of God, much less be inconsistent with it. Both here and in Rom. iii. 24, he mentions both in the same breath. For it is God who has given His beloved Son to be our Redeemer; it is of His undeserved favour that we are in Him; and the forgiveness that is granted is to us a free gift, though it cost Christ His blood to make it possible. If there is grace exhibited in our Lord's parable of the father receiving into his arms the returning prodigal, surely, when we know that there is in the reality, along with that, the love of the Shepherd seeking and suffering for His lost sheep, we may be convinced that, though it could not all be represented in any one image, there is, in our having redemption through Christ's blood, the remission of our trespasses, not only grace, but riches of grace, grace in giving Christ for us, grace in uniting us to Him, grace in accepting His redemption for us, and grace in freely forgiving us in Him.

8. which he made to abound (*or* wherewith he abounded) toward us] The verb in this clause is properly a neuter; but it is sometimes used in N. T. in a transitive sense (as 1 Thess. iii. 12): so it may have grace for its object, "which he made to abound." But possibly Paul's thought was the bolder one, that in respect of his grace God Himself abounded, poured Himself out, as it were, towards us. Probably he was careless about the construction, because God's grace is just God showing grace, the gracious God.

in all wisdom and prudence;] These words are so placed that they might be understood of attributes of God exercised in the work of our salvation; and some have thought this to be |the meaning. But the expression "all" is hardly appropriate in reference to God, and "prudence" more naturally refers to a human quality. It seems, therefore, more probable that Paul means that God in His abounding grace bestows these qualities on us. Thus, in addition to the blessing of forgiveness, there is mentioned that of enlightenment. Wisdom is specially a quality of the reason, or faculty by which we apprehend first principles, whether of knowledge or of practice, and denotes a clear and correct insight into these: prudence belongs to the understanding, or faculty of comparison, by which we draw inferences and adapt means to ends, and denotes a right use of that faculty to direct our actions.

9 prudence; having made known unto us the mystery of his will, according to his good pleasure which he hath purposed 10 in himself: that in the dispensation of the fulness of times he might gather together in one all things in Christ, both which are in heaven, and which are on earth; *even* in him:

9. **having made known unto us the mystery of his will,**] The word "mystery" in N. T. has a meaning different from that which it conveys now, when it commonly denotes something so great or difficult that we cannot understand or explain it, even when it is told to us. There are undoubtedly such things contained in the Bible; but the word mystery is often used when nothing of that kind is meant. It means simply a secret, something that has been hid, and that cannot be known except by revelation; though, when it is revealed, it may not be beyond our power to comprehend. Sometimes it is some truth or fact not yet made known; sometimes the hidden meaning of a parable or sign (so Matt. xiii. 11; Rev. i. 20, xvii. 7). In every case the word "secret" conveys the real meaning. So here Paul describes God as having made known to Christians the secret of His will, that design of His which had been hidden hitherto, but now was unveiled to them. What that is, the following clause indicates.

according to his good pleasure which he purposed in him] As in ver. 5, good pleasure conveys the idea of benevolence rather than that of mere sovereign appointment; and as Paul is going back at this point to the eternal purpose of God, "in him" may be taken as referring to Christ, though it may also be read "in himself." Though the revelation of God's grace has been only made in these last days, the grace itself is no afterthought of God, but has been purposed all along, from eternity.

10. **unto a dispensation of the fulness of the times** (*Gr. seasons*),] This shows that there was a wise reason for the delay. The fit season had not come for revealing God's grace: the race on which it was to be bestowed had been under age. This is the figure used by Paul in Gal. iv. 1–11; and he applies it not only to Israel, but to the Gentiles also. The heir is under guardians and stewards until the term appointed by the father: and the word "dispensation" here is "stewardship," or management of the house. God, the great house-Father, has fixed the term when the full blessings of His house are to be bestowed, and has so ordered the management of His household, that when the time is fully come, His great purpose of grace may be accomplished.

to sum up all things in Christ, the things in the heavens, and the things upon the earth;] The verb rendered "to sum up" is used by Paul, in the only other place where it occurs in N. T., Rom. xiii. 9, in reference to all the commandments being comprehended in the law of love: and in Heb. viii. 1, the noun from which it is formed is translated "sum" (A. V.), or "chief point" (R. V.). Here, however, it is not, as in these places, a number of declarations that are gathered up into one more general, but in the person of Christ the totality of beings are to be summed up or recapitulated. The meaning must therefore be that He is to represent all, and bind together all, not in a logical sense, but in a real way. Probably the apostle had in his mind the notion of "head" in the literal sense, as he elsewhere describes Christ as head over all things; but since the word he uses is derived not from that, but from "head" or "heading" in the logical

11 in whom also we have obtained an inheritance, being pre-

sense (as "head of a discourse," "heading of a chapter"), we cannot insist on that as distinctly taught here.

In the phrase "all things," Paul undoubtedly includes persons, though probably he did not mean to exclude even inanimate objects. It is the whole of created beings that he means, just as when he says, "all things were created through him" (Col. i. 16). They are also for Him; He has been appointed heir of all; they are all to be summed up in Him. This is what he asserts here, without explaining how this is to be done; and the more particular mention of "both the things in heaven and the things on earth" seems to be an employment of the familiar division of heaven and earth, as describing the whole universe. Among the things in heaven are doubtless the angels, and principalities, and powers, of which Paul speaks further on in this epistle; and from what he says there, we may learn his view of their relation to Christ: but the statement here is perfectly general, and only shows how great is that purpose of good will which God has formed in Him who is our Redeemer from sin.

The word Christ is here used, not simply as a proper name, as it had been hitherto, but, as is shown by its having the article, in its original official sense, the Messiah or Anointed of God, as if to indicate that it is in this capacity that all things are to be summed up in Him.

11. **in him, I say, in whom also we were made a heritage,**] The Authorised Version, "we have obtained an inheritance," represents a different translation of the same word; and as it occurs nowhere else in N. T., it is difficult to be certain which was the meaning intended. It is literally "we were allotted"; and just as the passive of similar verbs (*e.g.* entrust) may mean either "I was entrusted," or "I was entrusted with," *i.e.* something was entrusted to me: so this phrase may be construed either "we were allotted," *i.e.* assigned as a heritage (R. V.), or, we had a heritage allotted to us, *i.e.* obtained a heritage (A. V.). The words for lot in Hebrew and Greek, like our word, originally denoting the pebbles or other objects used for casting, in order to decide whose a thing should be, came to denote the thing itself so assigned; and since, when Israel entered the land of Caanan, the land to be possessed by each tribe and family was determined by lot, and secured by law inalienably to their descendants, the notion of a heritage became connected with the word. These hereditary lands were regarded as a portion from God, which it was impious to alienate (see 1 Kings xxi. 3). And as God was the giver of the earthly inheritance, the godly Israelite rose to the thought that Jehovah Himself was his portion, and would provide for him joy and blessing even beyond this life (see Ps. xvi. 5-11). Hence the blessings of God's people came to be spoken of as an inheritance; and this is the reference of the word here, according to the construction preferred by King James' translators. This is the meaning of "our inheritance" (ver. 14). But that verse also contains an allusion to another O. T. idea, which explains and gives countenance to the construction preferred by the Revisers. God speaks of having made Israel His portion or inheritance (Deut. iv. 20, "the Lord hath taken you . . . to be unto him a people of inheritance"); and in Jer. x. 16 the two ideas are expressed together: "The portion of Jacob is not like these: for he is the former of all things; and Israel is the tribe of his inheritance." This is just a special form of expressing the idea that runs through the whole

destinated according to the purpose of him who worketh all
12 things after the counsel of his own will : that we should be to

O. T., that God has chosen one nation to be His own special property: though all the earth is His, Israel has been redeemed to be a kingdom of priests, and a holy nation (Ex. xx. 5, 6). This is the idea implied in the designation holy, which Paul at the very outset of this epistle had applied to his readers along with himself (vers. 1, 4); and it is not unnatural that he should here introduce that special aspect of it which the prophets had expressed by saying that God had taken Israel to be His inheritance. The rendering of the Revised Version seems, therefore, on the whole to deserve the preference; "in Christ we were made a heritage," as Israel had been of old, only in a deeper and more spiritual sense.

Most interpreters think that at this point Paul passes, without signalising it, from the general use of "we," by which hitherto he had meant himself and his fellow-Christians as a whole, to a narrower application of it, to the believing Jews as distinguished from the Gentiles, among whom he includes his readers, addressing them as "ye" (ver. 13). The chief reason for this is the word "before hoped" in ver. 12. This view would also explain why he introduces again a statement of God's foreordination, which might seem needless after what he had said in vers. 4, 5. For, having spoken of the dispensation of the fulness of the times to sum up all things in Christ, and being about to mention the different times at which Jews and Gentiles were called, he declares that not only the great end, but also all the steps in the dispensation that led to it, were ordained by God's purpose. It must, however, be acknowledged that this sudden and unprepared change in the reference of "we" is somewhat unnatural; and it is doubtful whether Paul would say of himself before his conversion that he hoped in Christ. The word "before" may refer to the second coming of Christ; and the clause literally is, "who *have* before hoped in Christ." Thus it might still refer to Christians as a whole; and the address in the second person that follows may simply be meant to indicate that those addressed, as well as others, were among the number of the saints of whom such glorious things are true. On the whole, I prefer this explanation.

having been foreordained according to the purpose of him who worketh all things after the counsel of his will;] The special foreordination of God's people to be His heritage is here connected with the universal counsel of His will, according to which He works all things. The general doctrine of the divine purpose is briefly this, that whatever God does in time He has from eternity purposed to do. This is clearly asserted in the last clause of this verse; while in the preceding one it is shown that the foreordination of men to be God's heritage is in accordance with that all-embracing plan; and thus not only the fact, but the time and manner and circumstances of it, are ordered by the all-wise God. Since counsel is mentioned, we see that the divine will does not act arbitrarily, or without a reason, though the reason is not always made known to us. When theologians speak of God's eternal election being absolute or unconditional, they do not mean that it is without a reason, but only that it does not depend on any foreseen merit or goodness in those who are its objects. But the counsel is of God's will, it is not an iron necessity or inexorable fate by which the dispensation of the fulness of the times is ordered, but a living God, "who made of one every nation of men to dwell on all the face of the earth, having

13 the praise of his glory, who first trusted in Christ.   In whom ye also *trusted*, after that ye heard the word of truth, the gospel of your salvation : in whom also, after that ye believed, 14 ye were sealed with that Holy Spirit of promise, which is

determined their appointed seasons, and the bounds of their habitation ; that they should seek God, if haply they might feel after him, and find him, though he is not far from each one of us " (Acts xvii. 26, 27).

12. **to the end that we should be unto the praise of his glory, we who had (*or* have) before hoped in Christ:**] The purpose here expressed is that for which God has chosen a people as His heritage ; it had been declared by Him through the prophet, "this people have I formed for myself: they shall show forth my praise" (Isa. xliii. 21) ; and it is involved in the conception of a kingdom of priests, for priests are men set apart for the worship of God, and for bringing others also near to Him.   Israel was chosen and blessed by God, not for their own sake, but to be a light and a blessing to all the families of the earth.   The mass of the Jews had forgotten this, and thought that God's purpose was simply to bless them, and that all the natural descendants of Israel as such would possess the inheritance.   Paul tacitly sets aside that view, and indicates the true reason of their privileges. Their distinction is not physical descent, but that they had before hoped in the Messiah.   This phrase aptly describes the faith of the O. T. saints. It was a hope beforehand of a Saviour not yet actually come, looking not to a definite historical person, as would be indicated by the proper name "Jesus Christ," but to the Christ, the promised son of David, and servant of Jehovah, the same in whom Paul had said before, God is to sum up all things (ver. 10).

13. **in whom ye also, having heard the word of the truth, the gospel of your salvation,—in whom, having also believed, ye were sealed with the Holy Spirit of promise,**]   The dash (—) in the middle of this verse shows that the sense is either interrupted, or not completely expressed.   Some think that, as Paul sometimes, in a long and involved sentence, breaks off a clause that he has begun, and makes a fresh start by repeating the opening words (as in Rom. v. 12, 18 ; Eph. iii. 1, iv. 1), so here the second "in whom" is merely a repetition of the first ; but the intervening clause here is not so long as to make such an interruption natural, especially in a sentence where Paul has been carrying on a whole series of such clauses without finding any such interruption necessary.   It seems more probable, therefore, that some verb is meant to be understood to complete the sense of the first clause.   This, however, can hardly be "trusted" or "hoped" (as in A. V.) ; because that would be taking one part only of the compound participle, "before hoped" ; and it seems better to go back to the nearest verb in the indicative, "were made a heritage" (ver. 11), which also expresses the principal thought in the passage.   In Christ, says Paul, ye also, to whom I am writing, have been made God's heritage ; for though ye were strangers to the previous hope of Israel, ye have heard the word of truth, which has been to you glad tidings of salvation.   Two things are thus emphasised about the Christian message : its certain truth, for without that it could not be relied on for such momentous issues ; and its welcome character, as bringing glad news of deliverance from sin and misery.

Then the next clause adds a new thought, how this gospel was confirmed

the earnest of our inheritance until the redemption of the
15 purchased possession, unto the praise of his glory. Wherefore
in their personal experience; this, too, like all the blessings of salvation, being
in Christ. "Having believed, ye were sealed with the Spirit" might also be
rendered "when ye believed," as the same phrase is in Acts xix. 2; for it
does not imply that the believing was earlier in time than the sealing. The
gift of the Holy Spirit, in the experience of Christians, ordinarily comes in and
with faith (see Gal. iii. 2, 5, 14), though Paul also teaches that there is an
agency of the Spirit that is the cause of faith, for no man can say Jesus is
Lord, but in the Holy Spirit (1 Cor. xii. 3; cf. ii. 4–16).

The idea of a seal is a token or mark, and as applied to believers it is
something given them to show, to themselves and others, that they are the
people of God. Abraham received the sign of circumcision as a seal of the
righteousness of faith (Rom. iv. 11); but our seal is not anything external.
Ye were sealed with the Spirit of promise, that is, the Spirit whose outpouring
and sanctifying agency had been promised by the prophets (Isa. xxxii. 15–17,
xliv. 3, 5; Ezek. xxxvi. 27; Joel ii. 28), and by Jesus Himself; and the character
of the Spirit and His work, as morally good, is brought out by the adjective "the
holy," placed emphatically at the end. This makes it probable that the
reference is not to any extraordinary gifts, such as tongues or prophecy, but
to the moral qualities, such as truth, love, purity, by which believers in Jesus
were marked out.

14. which is an earnest of our inheritance, unto the redemption of
God's own possession, unto the praise of his glory.] An earnest is more
than a seal or pledge, because it is actually part of what is to be bestowed in
due time. The word is a commercial one, probably coming from the
Phœnicians, the great merchant nation of antiquity, from whom it was
borrowed by the Greeks and Romans; it is the same as the Scottish *arles*.
The graces of the Spirit, its fruit of love, joy, peace, and the rest, are not
only a strong assurance that we are Christ's, but a foretaste of the perfect
blessedness that is in store for us. Grace is just glory begun, and glory is
grace perfected. So Paul says (Rom. viii. 23) we have received the first-
fruits of the Spirit, *i.e.* the Spirit which is the firstfruits of the glory that is
to be revealed. Here it is called our inheritance, but in the same breath we
are called God's own possession, the two ideas being combined, as in Jer. x. 16,
and now, too, Jews and Gentiles are no longer distinguished; both in Christ
having the same earnest and inheritance.

The A. V. "of the purchased possession" was, according to the use
of language in its day, more literal than R. V.; for "to purchase" did
not mean then to buy or obtain for payment, but simply to acquire;
and the word in the original denotes not merely a possession, but one
that has been acquired. It is derived from the word used in Acts xx. 28,
"the church of God, which he purchased with his own blood," where the
idea of buying, if it is included at all, is conveyed, not by the word "purchased,"
but by the clause following. The idea here is that believers in Jesus, gathered
from among Jews and Gentiles, are a people over whom God has acquired a
special right, as a heritage of His own; but He has not yet actually taken them
to Himself; they are in the world, where they are exposed to rival claims and
hostile assaults: the ransom has been given for them; but they are not yet
fully delivered from this present evil world: the day of redemption is that
when the full effect of the ransom shall be accomplished, and the Saviour shall

I also, after I heard of your faith in the Lord Jesus, and love
16 unto all the saints, cease not to give thanks for you, making
17 mention of you in my prayers; that the God of our Lord

see of the travail of His soul, and shall be satisfied. Meanwhile the people of God are marked as His by the seal of the Holy Spirit; and in the day when He maketh up His jewels (the same word as "possession" here), He shall claim them all, and triumphantly bring them home to the praise of His glory.

I. 15–II. 10. *Prayer for Believers.*—After this great outbreak of praise, Paul goes on, as is his wont, to express his thankfulness for the Christian faith of his readers, and his prayer for its increase. This he does in another long sentence, which extends in an unbroken series of connected clauses to the end of the chapter; and even then is interrupted only grammatically, for the connection of thought goes on without break to ch. ii. 10.

15. **For this cause I also, having heard of the faith in the Lord Jesus which is among (*or* in) you, and [the love] which** *ye shew* **toward all the saints,**] Paul's saying, that he had heard of their faith, is consistent with the view that he did not personally know them; but it does not necessarily imply that, for he uses the same word to Philemon, who was his own convert (Philem. 5, 19). Still it is more like his address to the Colossians, whom he had not visited, than that to the Philippians, whom he had. The words "the love," which have been banished to the margin in R. V., are wanting in the oldest MSS., though found in all the ancient versions. The question is a difficult and doubtful one; but if they are omitted, the presence of the definite article seems to require the translation to be, "the faith in the Lord Jesus which is among you, and that which is toward all the saints." Faith would thus appear to be used in the second reference for faithfulness. The word bears both meanings, and Paul sometimes passes from the one to the other (*e.g.* Rom. iii. 3; 1 Thess. iii. 2, 3). In Philem. 5, his faith, or faithfulness, is described as "toward the Lord Jesus, and toward all the saints"; and that expression in a contemporary epistle gives countenance to the reading that omits "love" here.

16. **cease not to give thanks for you, making mention** *of you* **in my prayers**;] This statement is connected with the preceding by "therefore," which refers to the whole great doxology (vers. 3–14). Because God has bestowed on us such blessings, in such a wonderful way, Paul feels impelled to give thanks for all whom he knows or hears to have been brought to faith in Christ, and so made partakers of these blessings; and in his personal devotion he remembers, and commends to God, the various communities of believers in different parts of the world. While he gives thanks, he also prays on their behalf for what they still need; for their salvation is only begun by their being united to Christ in faith, and needs both prayer and effort that it may be brought to completion. Thus naturally praise passes into thanksgiving, and thanksgiving into petition. It is instructive, too, to observe the variety and appropriateness of Paul's prayers for the different churches to which he wrote. His intercessions were not merely general and formal, but suited to the circumstances and wants of each. For the Thessalonians, who were new converts among heathen immorality, he prays that they may be strengthened in holiness (1 Thess. iii. 11–13). Of the Galatians he stands in doubt, and travails in spirit till Christ be formed in them. For the Romans he prays that he may

Jesus Christ, the Father of glory, may give unto you the
spirit of wisdom and revelation in the knowledge of him:
18 the eyes of your understanding being enlightened; that ye

be prospered to come to them and impart some spiritual gift that they may
be strengthened (Rom. i. 10, 11). For the Colossians, and here, he prays for
true spiritual knowledge, probably because they were in danger of being led
astray after a false knowledge.

17. that the God of our Lord Jesus Christ, the Father of glory, may
give unto you a spirit of wisdom and revelation in the knowledge of
him;] He invokes God here not as the Father of our Lord Jesus Christ (as he
often does), nor as both his God and Father (as in ver. 3), but as his God. For
all through vers. 20–23, everything that God is said to have done for Christ is
done as His God. Our Saviour is contemplated as the Christ, the Servant of
Jehovah; and God's power and glory are seen in what He did for Him, and
for us in Him. But God is also addressed as the Father of glory, a peculiar
expression, which is not to be diluted into "the glorious Father," nor "the
author of glory," but is rather "the Father who gives glory." He is the
Father absolutely; and as the God of the incarnate Son, He is contemplated as
the giver of glory, first to Christ, and then to us in Him (cf. Acts iii. 13, "the
God of our fathers hath glorified his servant Jesus").

The translation "a spirit of wisdom and revelation" in R. V. is hardly
necessary, and the word cannot be understood of the human spirit; for though
to give a spirit of wisdom would be a biblical expression for giving wisdom
to our spirit, we could not take "a spirit of revelation" to mean a spirit that
receives revelation. The reference is rather to the Spirit of God, viewed in
the special character of the giver of wisdom and revelation. Though Paul
had just said that they had been sealed with the Holy Spirit, referring
especially to the love, joy, and peace that accompany faith, he knew that
they could not yet have attained the full measure of knowledge that he
desired they should have; and, recognising the Spirit of God as the giver of
this also, he prays that God would give them the Spirit in this special
character and work. Wisdom is, as in ver. 8, the capacity to apprehend truths
above the reach of sense; and revelation is the discovery to us of the things of
God. The application of this word is not restricted by Paul, as it often is in
our use of it, to the communication of extraordinary messages; but it denotes
a special agency of the Holy Spirit opening up to us the mind and will of
God.

The way in which he desires the bestowal of these gifts, and looks for
them to appear, is in the full knowledge of Him, *i.e.*, as the following explanation shows, of God. Some knowledge of Him they undoubtedly had; but
he prays that they may have more, especially in regard to the three things
mentioned in vers. 18, 19.

18. having the eyes of your heart enlightened,] This illustrates the
gift of wisdom and revelation for which he prays. It gives light to the
inward sight. "The eyes of the heart" is a peculiar expression, but not
difficult to understand. The heart, in biblical language, does not denote
especially the seat of the emotions, it is often used to describe the faculty of
knowledge, and it is never opposed, as commonly with us, to the head or the
mind: its counterpart in Scripture is rather the hands, or the mouth, or the
appearance; and so it denotes all that is inward, as distinguished from what

may know what is the hope of his calling, and what the
19 riches of the glory of his inheritance in the saints, and what
is outward. So here it is the mental and spiritual power of vision that is to
receive light by the gift of God's Spirit.

that ye may know what is the hope of his calling,] Paul's prayer
for their enlightenment is in general that they may know what is involved in
their Christianity. This is in substance the same object that John tells us he
had in view in his general epistle, "that ye may know that ye have eternal
life, who believe on the name of the Son of God" (1 John v. 13). Direct
faith in Christ brings us into the state of salvation; but the believer is not at
first conscious of all that is implied in that, and growth in Christian life
consists largely in coming to see all that we have in Christ, and to enter into
the enjoyment of the blessings, and fulfilment of the duties, of life, in Him.
This knowledge is more particularly presented here in three aspects; but
these are not to be looked upon as so many separate objects; for they are all
comprehended in "the knowledge of him" (ver. 17), and each involves the others.
We should fail to realise our Christian standing if we thought of God either
as giving no hope to such as we are, or as taking no personal interest in us, or
as leaving us to our own strength, which is but weakness. But by what God
has done for Christ, and for us in Him, we get such a knowledge of Him, as
assures us we need fear none of these things.

God's calling is what Paul had referred to above (ver. 13), when he spoke of
their having heard the word of truth as glad tidings of their salvation; and
now he would have them know what hope this calling should and does
awaken. If they had regarded it at first as merely offering them deliverance
from a state of misery, he would have them see that it promises them also the
richest blessings, so that they do not need to have recourse for Christian
perfection to any higher knowledge or discipline, different from the gospel
which they had received, and supplementary to the salvation that is in
Christ.

what the riches of the glory of his inheritance in the saints,]
Many expositors think that by "his inheritance" here Paul expresses the
same idea as when he says we are "heirs of God" (Rom. viii. 17). But on
that view the words "in the saints" present a difficulty, which has received a
variety of explanations, none of them very satisfactory. On the other hand,
"God's inheritance" is a frequent O. T. phrase (see Deut. iv. 20, ix. 29, xxxii.
9; Ps. xxviii. 9, lxxviii. 71), describing the chosen people Israel as God's special
possession; and the idea of their being holy is correlative to this one (see
Ex. xix. 5, 6; Deut. xiv. 2, etc.), so that "God's inheritance in the saints"
more naturally suggests the thought of the saints, or holy ones, being themselves the property or heritage of God. This thought is indicated by the word
"possession" in ver. 14; and if the Revised Version is correct, has been
expressed in ver. 11, "we were made a heritage." So Paul would be here
pointing back to that, and desiring that they might know what was implied
in it. That God counts us as His own possession, is really a more wonderful
thought than that we are to enjoy Him as our portion, and the knowledge of
what it implies is more fitted to be encouraging and stimulating in Christian
life. It might seem to the early converts, that the community they had
joined was but poor and mean, even though it had a gospel of salvation. But
Paul would have them know that it was God's own heritage, for which He
cared, and which He would make abundantly glorious. The glory of God's

is the exceeding greatness of his power to us-ward who believe, according to the working of his mighty power, 20 which he wrought in Christ, when he raised him from the

inheritance is the honour and beauty for which He has destined His people, that they should be holy and without blemish before Him; and the riches of that glory is the fulness, abundance, preciousness of that honour and beauty.

19. **and what the exceeding greatness of his power to us-ward who believe,**] As the preceding clause points to their knowing how deeply God is concerned to bring His people to the utmost beauty and honour; this one desires that they might also understand how perfectly able He is to accomplish this; how great, surpassing all measure, is the power of God towards, *i.e.* exerted upon, us who believe. The way in which this power acts is shown afterwards in ch. ii. 4–11; and from that it appears that it is not of the nature of mere physical omnipotence, but divine influence working in the moral and spiritual world, giving new life, deliverance from sin, and activity in godliness. Here, though not in the previous clauses, Paul inserts "us who believe," and the reason may perhaps be, that while the glory of God's inheritance may be known by seeing it in others, the greatness of His power can only be appreciated by experiencing it in ourselves.

20. **according to that working of the strength of his might which he wrought in Christ,**] This declares the measure by which the greatness of God's power towards us may be estimated, and the clause should be connected with the main thought in the preceding: "that ye may know the greatness of God's power toward us to be according to that working of the strength of his might which he wrought in Christ." The three words here used express very emphatically the power of God. That which is rendered "might" is inherent power, as an attribute of God; "strength" refers to that power coming forth into exercise; and "working" describes it as producing its effect. "Which he hath wrought in the Messiah;" so the clause, according to the best authorities, may be literally rendered, for it refers to a great act done once for all, the effect of which is continually present, and it designates our Saviour, not by His personal proper name, but by His title, as the Lord's anointed, the King and representative of His people. It was in this capacity that He was exalted: and the power manifested in His exaltation is not fully seen, unless it be remembered that He was raised, not merely as an individual, but as the Messiah. For the same reason probably it is that Paul says, not merely "on him," but "in him." The raising of the dead to life is indeed an act of superhuman power, which is frequently spoken of in O. T. as a special prerogative of God. But in raising the dead Christ, God has not only exerted that physical omnipotence, but a far more wonderful moral power, casting out the prince of this world, triumphing over the powers of evil, delivering men from the guilt of sin, and begetting them again to a living hope of an eternal inheritance.

Paul has now completed his statement of what he prayed that his readers might be spiritually enlightened to know; but as this has ended in a reference to the divine power exerted in Christ, he goes on, without interrupting the sentence begun at ver. 15, to describe the various stages and aspects of our Lord's exaltation; and so passes imperceptibly, as he does also in his epistle to the Colossians, from thanksgiving and prayer for them, to teaching addressed to them.

dead, and set *him* at his own right hand in the heavenly
21 *places*, far above all principality, and power, and might, and
dominion, and every name that is named, not only in this

when he raised him from the dead, and made him to sit at his right hand in the heavenly *places*,] The state from which God raised Him is the lowest possible, that of the dead, those who are deprived of all earthly activity and perception, and who have come into that state by the judgment of God on account of sin. So Paul undoubtedly conceived of death, following the O. T. ideas; and he regarded the death of Christ as our redemption from sin, and death as its wages. He was made a curse for us; but He was Himself sinless, and so He was among the dead only because He was the head and representative of sinners. In raising Him, therefore, God not merely exercised the physical power of giving life to a dead body, but cancelled the guilt of sin, and redeemed all who are in Christ from its power. The word "raised" here is often used for awaking out of sleep or trance, and may perhaps indicate that Christ could not be holden of death, though He freely condescended to come under its power for our sakes.

In extreme contrast to this is the state to which God has exalted Him, as expressed in the clause, "and seated him at his right hand in the heavenlies." This phrase, taken from Ps. cx. 1, and from the words which Jesus is recorded to have spoken at His trial before the Sanhedrin (Matt. xxvi. 64; Mark xv. 62; Luke xxii. 69), is not intended to describe any locality in the material universe, but the supreme honour and dominion with which Christ has been invested. He is not simply brought before God, as the figure like a Son of man in Dan. vii. 13, He is placed beside God, on the right, the place of honour, over against the created universe, which is before God; He is seated, as having finished His work, and entered into abiding glory. It means, in a word, that our Lord, the man Christ Jesus, is adored with God, and rules with God over all.

21. **far above all rule, and authority, and power, and dominion, and every name that is named, not only in this world (*or* age), but also in that which is to come :**] These words amplify the assertion of the supreme exaltation of Christ, and serve to give a more vivid idea of it, by mentioning various superhuman powers over which He has been set. For it appears, from comparing this with later passages in this epistle (chs. iii. 10, vi. 12), as well as with Rom. viii. 38, that angelic beings are meant; though Paul's object is not to inform us about the ranks and gradations of these, but simply to assure us that all are subject to Christ. The R. V. of the first pair, "rule and authority," is not very happy, because in chs. iii. 10 and vi. 12 these very same words are rendered, as in A. V., "principalities and powers"; and they clearly mean, here as there, not the abstract rule, but beings who exercise rule and authority. They are sometimes used for earthly sovereigns and magistrates who exercise rule and authority; and here they seem to point to something analogous in the angelic world. They may refer to the guardian angels of nations, referred to in certain mysterious passages of O. T., Dan. x. 13, 20, 21; Deut. xxxii. 8 (LXX.); and there is no evidence that they refer to any rule or authority over other angels, though that is a possible supposition. Of the other two words, "power" is frequently used for host, in the expressions "host of God," "Lord of hosts," and the like in O. T.; it describes, not right or authority, but the force by which such

22 world, but also in that which is to come: and hath put all
things under his feet, and gave him *to be* the head over all

authority is carried into effect; while "dominion" denotes the lordship or command by which that force is wielded.

From this passage, along with Col. i. 16, the mystic theologians of the Middle Ages drew their fanciful speculations about the divisions and ranks of the angelic hierarchy, which they arranged in nine degrees, or three classes of three each. But all this is just of a piece with that reverencing of angels and intruding into things unseen, against which Paul warns the Colossians. When we compare the names and the order in which they occur in the different places, we find it impossible to recognise any regular gradation, whether we take them in an ascending or in a descending scale; and the apostle's meaning seems simply to be, that whatever may be the greatness and dignity of superhuman beings, Christ is above them all, and we have to do directly with Him, and need not have recourse, for the perfection of our spiritual life, to any intermediate agency. Here, however, his purpose is not directly controversial, though he had this thought in his mind.

The last clause of ver. 21 completes the thought. "Name" suggests the idea of honour, as the previous words had indicated power. Christ is not only invested with supreme rule, He is crowned with glory above all renown that ever has been or shall be attained by any. Many names are remembered and made mention of before God, for great and good service done to Him in this age; many more may be even more renowned in the age that is to come, after Christ's glorious return; but far above every one of them, even the worthiest, the name of Christ is exalted.

22. **And he put all things in subjection under his feet, and gave him to be head over all things to the church,**] The first clause is a quotation from Ps. viii. 6, which Paul had also made in 1 Cor. xv. 27, and which is more fully cited and explained in Heb. ii. 6, 9. The psalm refers to the honour and dominion which God has bestowed on man; and Paul sees that this is not fully realised in the race as we actually know it, but in the exaltation of Him who called Himself the Son of Man, who is the last Adam, the second Man, the new representative of mankind, he regards the Psalmist's word as virtually fulfilled, while it is to be really and perfectly fulfilled, in due time, in all who are His.

Having now brought to a climax his description of the exaltation of Christ, Paul declares, with a brevity that is emphatic by contrast with the preceding fulness of statement, that God has given this so gloriously exalted Christ to the Church. Here first in this epistle we meet with this memorable word, after the way had been prepared for it by the mention of God's calling (ver. 18). For the word denotes the assembly of those who are called out; and they, as here described, are those who are "holy and believers in Christ," who have also been designated God's heritage or possession. The word *ecclesia*, which we render "church," came into use to describe the Christian society, because it had been previously employed as a translation of that which is generally rendered "congregation" in English, as applied in O. T. to the people of Israel. Another rendering of that word was "synagogue," which was applied, not only to the people as a whole, but to the various sections of it who met for common worship, especially when these were scattered among heathens in foreign lands. As the Christian assemblies were formed after the model of the synagogues, it was natural that the same

23 *things* to the church, which is his body, the fulness of him that filleth all in all.

should be applied to them, and should become current in the form (*ecclesia*) most familiar to Greeks. It first appears as a designation of the several congregations of believers in Christ gathered in various places; but in this epistle, and that to the Colossians, Paul conceives of all the believers forming one community, which was the real people and heritage of God, the continuation under the new covenant of the true Israel of the older dispensation. It was a bold conception to form of the small scattered and isolated societies of believers in Jesus; but it flowed from Paul's fundamental doctrine, that salvation in the kingdom of God depended not on natural descent from Abraham and observance of the law, but on a birth of the Spirit and faith in Jesus Christ. How it flowed from this, we see, *e.g.*, in Gal. iv. 21–31, where the apostle's illustration of the freedom of the gospel leads him to the thought of the Jerusalem which is above, which is our mother, in contrast with the Jerusalem that now is, *i.e.* the existing religious community of Israel. In his later epistles he naturally speaks more of the Church as a whole; and here he says that God has given Christ as head over all things to it. The "all things" here must have the same universal reference as in the previous clause, and the expression "head over all things" probably points back to the purpose mentioned (ver. 10) to sum up all things in Christ. He who is head over all things by supreme dominion is given to be head of the Church in a more special and intimate way, as is asserted in what follows.

23. **which is his body, the fulness of him that filleth all in all.**] The relative "which" here implies that the clause introduced by it gives a ground for the preceding, and amounts to "which indeed," or "since it is his body." Christ's dominion over all things is a headship of the Church, inasmuch as it is His body. He is head *over* the universe, because He is its absolute Lord and governor; but He is head *of* the Church, because it stands in a vital relation to Him, as the members of the natural body do to the head.

This is explained in the last clause, in which Paul introduces another expression of frequent occurrence in this and the Colossian epistle, "fulness." But the precise meaning is difficult to ascertain, since the word may be variously construed. The fulness of a thing most commonly means that with which it is filled, *e.g.* "the earth is the Lord's, and the fulness thereof"; and thus many have thought Paul's idea to be that the Church, as Christ's body, is that with which He is filled, or made complete, the complement, as the other members are to the head, making up the entire body. But fulness may mean that which is filled, *e.g.* "basketfuls of broken pieces" (Mark viii. 20); and many think that it is to be understood here as meaning that which is filled with Christ, or God. The decision between these two views depends partly on the interpretation of the following words, which is also questionable. The verb "filleth" may be taken as a passive "is filled"; and the object "all" could be understood as "with all things" (as "filled with the fruit of righteousness," Phil. i. 11); but the following "in all" would hardly admit of explanation on this view. For this and other reasons, it is now generally agreed that the active rendering "filleth" is preferable. "All" cannot naturally be taken in any less extensive sense than the "all things" in the preceding verses, *i.e.* the whole universe; and "in all" may mean in all respects, or with all (benefits), or more literally, being in all. The statement is thus equivalent to that in ch. iv. 10, that Christ "ascended far above all

CHAP. II. 1. And you *hath he quickened*, who were dead
2 in trespasses and sins; wherein in time past ye walked

the heavens that he might fill all things," where it is plain that the meaning is *fill*, not by putting something else into that which is filled, but by occupying it Himself. The words "in all," added here, serve to show that He not only occupies the whole universe as such, but is present in each of the beings of which it is composed. Thus the whole verse would mean, either "the Church is the body of Christ, and belongs to the completeness of Him who fills with His presence the universe in all its parts"; or "the Church is the body of Christ, and filled with the presence of Him who also fills the universe in all its parts." On the former view, the last clause is added to show that, though in a sense Christ is made full by the Church, yet at the same time it, and all things, are filled with His presence: we are in Him, but He is also in us. On the latter view, the last clause would simply say that Christ fills with His indwelling, not only the Church, but the universe in all its parts. This would seem to weaken somewhat the privilege asserted of the Church, by making the being filled with Christ a truth that can be asserted of all things. On this and on grammatical grounds the former explanation is perhaps preferable, though the latter is more generally adopted.

Paul has now illustrated the greatness of God's power in the exaltation of Christ as head of the Church. But what he desired his readers to know was its greatness as exerted on themselves who believed; and accordingly he goes on to describe how they had been raised from a state of spiritual death to life in Christ.

II. 1. And you *did he quicken*, when ye were dead through your trespasses and sins,] The words "did he quicken" are not in the original, but only inserted from ver. 5 for the sake of the sense. But the abruptness of Paul's style would be better represented by omitting them, and no real obscurity would be caused. The apostle draws, in vers. 1-3, a picture of their former state, unrelieved by any mention of their deliverance: the conjunction "and" connects this with the statement in ch. i. 20, "he raised Christ from the dead"; and then, at ver. 4, the sentence is broken off and resumed in a more emphatic form. Here, then, there is only the state of death to be considered: the giving of life comes after.

Some think that by "dead" is meant doomed to die, as being under condemnation, and that what the apostle is about to describe is deliverance from the guilt of sin, and introduction into the favour and fellowship of God. The phrase may have that meaning; but it is more natural to understand it, as most interpreters have done, of a moral state which, later in this epistle (ch. iv. 18), is expressed by the words "alienated from the life of God," *i.e.* having no real correspondence with God as our environment, no sense of His presence, no apprehension of His discoveries of Himself, no exercise of mind or affections towards Him.

"Through your trespasses and sins" expresses the idea more exactly than "in"; for they are represented not as the state in which this death to God exists, but rather as the cause by which it has come. God did not make man without capacity for life to Him; but He made him such that by his sin he might lose it; and Paul teaches elsewhere that all mankind have lost it through the transgression of Adam. Yet this does not exclude the recognition implied here, that it is through trespasses and sins of their own that men are dead to God. "Trespasses" refer to various acts of unright-

according to the course of this world, according to the prince of the power of the air, the spirit that now
3 worketh in the children of disobedience: among whom

eousness; "sins," to various forms in which evil habits and dispositions appear.

2. wherein aforetime ye walked according to the course (*Gr.* age) of this world, according to the prince of the power of the air, of the spirit that now worketh in the sons of disobedience;] This clause shows that, though dead to God, they were not destitute of activity in other relations. There was an environment with which they had correspondence, but a very sad and terrible one. They had been walking, proceeding in a career of voluntary action in their trespasses and sins; and the influences that directed that walk are described as being the world around them, and superhuman powers of evil. "This world" here means, not the material universe in its order and beauty, but the mass of mankind as living for things seen, and not for God; and the age or course of it is the time now passing in which its ungodly tendencies prevail and increase. That might be discerned, by any careful observer, to be an influence by which men were swept along in a course of immorality. But Paul saw, behind and above that, an agency which he calls "the prince of the power of the air." There can be no doubt that he thus designates him whom further on in this epistle he calls "the devil" (chs. iv. 26, vi. 11); and who is elsewhere called "the prince of this world." But the name here given him occurs nowhere else; and the reference to the air is somewhat perplexing, and has led to much discussion and variety of opinion. The simplest explanation seems to be, that it describes the region in which the devil has sway, as above the earth but beneath the heavenly places, in which Paul had just said Christ has been seated far above all principality and power (ch. i. 21). The words here used, "prince of the power," correspond to these, and indicate one of the princes and authorities above which our Lord has been exalted, and above which, as is said presently (ver. 6), believers are exalted in Him. But over this world that prince of evil reigns, and is represented as having forces at his command, such as are more fully described in ch. vi. 11. The word here rendered "power" means authority, and seems to be used in a collective sense, for the whole of the supermundane forces of evil that are under the leadership of the prince of this world. In the following clause, "the spirit that now worketh in the sons of disobedience," cannot grammatically be identified with the prince, but must refer either to "the authority" or to "the air," and most naturally to the former. The supermundane forces under their prince are a spirit working in men's hearts. This is made more vivid by being described in its present activity. Ye aforetime walked under this influence, from which ye have been graciously delivered; but, alas! it is still ruling in many of your fellows, who have not obeyed the divine call. "Sons of disobedience" is a Hebraistic phrase, and is to be regarded not merely as a periphrasis for the simple adjective "disobedient," but as intensifying the meaning, those who belong to disobedience, are in its clutches, so to say. There may be a special reference to unbelief as disobedience to the gospel, but in such a general description it cannot be limited to that; it includes disobedience to God's law as made known by nature and conscience, and the addition of this clause indicates that what-

also we all had our conversation in times past in the lusts of our flesh, fulfilling the desires of the flesh and of the mind: and were by nature the children of wrath, even as

ever may be the working of the evil spirit, it is only on those who are voluntarily disregarding their known duty that it takes effect.

The whole verse, thus understood, without satisfying any vain curiosity, or exhibiting any superstitious fancy, conveys moral and religious truths that have important practical bearings; that the prevalence of immorality among mankind is due not only to evil fashions, customs, or examples, but to a dark superhuman power; that this power is not supreme or equal to the divine, but belongs to an intermediate though supermundane region; and that it can gain control over men only through their disobedience to God. Thus, while it teaches us not to underestimate the enormous power of evil in the world, it also assures us that it is not invincible, and gives an indication, which is afterwards more fully explained, how it is to be resisted and overcome.

3. among whom we also all once lived (A. V. had our conversation) in the lusts of our flesh, doing the desires of the flesh and of the mind (*Gr.* thoughts), and were by nature children of wrath, even as the rest:] Paul now widens his description, so as to include himself and all his fellow-believers along with those he is addressing. There is nothing in the context to suggest that he is speaking here in the name of the Jewish Christians as opposed to the Gentiles; his words are quite universal, "all we," who now through God's grace have been quickened to new life, once lived, *i.e.* moved about, had our conversation, in the old sense of that expression, moving to and fro in habitual intercourse. Among the sons of disobedience we all once spent our life, ruled not by the law of God, but by our own impulses, whether of a lower or of a higher kind. The lusts or desires of the flesh, in the more limited sense, denote animal appetites and passions; those of the thoughts are the desires that are formed through our intellectual and social nature, such as the love of beauty, of knowledge, of power, of wealth, and that "last infirmity of noble minds," the desire of fame. When speaking in his own name, Paul describes the inward side of the ungodly state, as known in conscious experience, while in his statement about others (ver. 2) he had only spoken of its outward aspect and relations, as a walking in actual and habitual sin under the influence of the world, and the evil spirits that rule the world.

Then he adds a clause, which is emphatic because it departs from the regular grammatical structure of the sentence, and instead of being introduced by a participle, like the former one, "and being," is made an independent assertion, "and we were by nature children of wrath, even as the rest." Though it is not said whose is the wrath, there can be no doubt that the apostle means the wrath of God, which he says elsewhere is revealed from heaven against all ungodliness and unrighteousness of men (Rom. i. 18), that is, the righteous indignation of the Holy One against all that is unholy and evil. "Children of wrath," like "sons of disobedience" in ver. 2, is a Hebraism, denoting those who belong to wrath, are justly under it. They who are sons of disobedience cannot but be children of wrath; as Paul says further on in this epistle (ch. v. 6), on account of their immorality "the wrath of God cometh on the sons of disobedience."

Such we all were, Paul says, "by nature," or birth. The word denotes

4 others. But God, who is rich in mercy, for his great love
5 wherewith he loved us, even when we were dead in sins,
hath quickened us together with Christ, (by grace ye are

that which is not made, but grows, and it shows that the sinful state that has just been described is not to be traced to any action in our individual lives, but is one in which we are born. That the power and prevalence of evil in our hearts and lives is due to a disorder of our moral constitution, which we have as we come into the world, was recognised by those who thought deeply and were taught by God to see their own sinfulness, even in O. T. times, as we see from such utterances as Ps. li., and it was taught more distinctly in proportion as the divine grace, that can alone remedy it, was more clearly revealed.

In the last clause, "even as the rest," Paul intimates that this terrible and deadly moral disorder extends to all men; and then he hastens to describe, in bright contrast to this awful picture, the wondrous love and rich grace of God, in which He delivers us from our death in sin. Indeed, the word " by nature " seems to have been introduced, not to give a more exact doctrinal formula, but to suggest the contrast of what we now are by God's grace.

4. but God, being rich in mercy, for his great love wherewith he loved us,] The number and strength of the expressions of God's gracious disposition towards us in this paragraph are very striking. Here are mercy and love, and further on, grace and kindness, and these repeated, and qualified with the strongest epithets; rich in mercy, great love, exceeding riches of grace. The belief that all men are by nature children of wrath, does not imply, as is sometimes supposed, a conception of God as mere sovereign power, that excludes love as the essence of His being. Clearly it did not do so in Paul's mind; for immediately after the dark view he has given of man's depravity, he exhausts the resources of language to exhibit the love of God in its various aspects. First we have mercy, *i.e.* pity for the suffering. God looks on mankind, dead through sins, with anger indeed, but at the same time with pity; and while He is never said to be rich in anger, He is declared to be rich in pity, so that He bestows it ungrudgingly on all His suffering creatures. Then Paul mentions, as the ground and motive of the great work of God that he is going to describe, His love, which he characterises as great, or more literally "much," and as wholly His own, not deserved by anything good, or attracted by anything fair, in its objects. The "us" here is defined in the following verse to be those who have been quickened with Christ; not that Paul would deny the pity and love of God to the rest of mankind, for he has elsewhere spoken as warmly of the riches of His goodness, and forbearance, and long-suffering towards the impenitent (Rom. ii. 4), and of His grace bringing salvation to all men, and His kindness and love to man (Tit. ii. 11, iii. 4); but here he is thinking of the great fact of the actual deliverance of himself and the other believers from the terrible state of death in sin, and he speaks especially of the great and wonderful love of God shown in that.

5. even when we were dead through our trespasses, quickened us together with Christ (by grace have ye been saved),] The first clause of this verse repeats and recalls ver. 1, and though grammatically it is connected with the following statement, serves to intensify rather the preceding

assertion of the love of God. The power exerted in bringing to life is not enhanced by the previous state of death, for that is implied in any case; but the love in which that power is put forth is seen to be more wonderful, from the fact that the objects of it were in the wretched and loathsome state of spiritual death. Yet even in this state God's love is strong enough to give us life. "Quickened" here, as elsewhere in the English Bible, has its old signification "made alive," as appears alike by its contrast to the death before described and now reasserted, and by its connection with the acts of life expressed in the following words. God communicates spiritual life to dead souls; and then calls it out into active and triumphant exercise.

The most striking thing here is that God is said to have made us alive "together with Christ," and not merely through or in Him. The difficulty of understanding this may have contributed, along with a natural slip in writing, to the insertion of "in," which is found in some ancient MSS. and versions; but the reading of the text is the best supported. Many interpreters have thought that this is to be understood as spoken, by way of anticipation, in reference to the future resurrection of the body, of which Paul says (1 Cor. xv. 22), "in Christ shall all be made alive." But here the tense, not of one only, but of three verbs, is too distinctly historical to make such an interpretation natural; and most modern expositors agree that Paul is describing the passage from death to life that takes place at conversion, and was a historical fact in the case of himself and his fellow-Christians. This Paul connects with God's quickening Christ from death, not only as its pattern and parallel, but also as its ground and means. The thought involved in this is explained in other passages where he speaks of the same subject, and expresses his ideas more fully. The nearest parallel is Col. ii. 11-15, from which we see that a preliminary to our being quickened with Christ is our dying and being buried with Him in baptism. That implies an acknowledgment that our old life was really death, and must come to an end in death. Christ's death on our behalf frees us from guilt and condemnation, and enables us to be done with that old life in death; and His being quickened from death secures for us a new life like His. The same thought is expressed in Rom. vi. 4-11, and the germ of it is found in Jesus' sayings, Matt. xvi. 24-26; John xii. 23-26. Jesus compared Himself to a grain of wheat falling into the ground and dying, that it might not remain alone, but bear much fruit. In His resurrection He sprang from the earth, and the fruits that He bears are the souls who, hating their life in this world, and following Him, have life eternal. The life that they receive is the same life to which Christ was raised, since, according to His other parable, they are branches in Him, the true vine; and Paul, combining the images of these parables, says: "If we have become one plant with him in the likeness of his death, we shall be also in the likeness of his resurrection" (Rom. vi. 5). We have been made spiritually alive, and the life that we have received is the same that the risen Saviour has; so that it may be truly said, we are quickened, not merely through Christ, but with Him; God's giving life from the dead to the seed, carried with it His giving life also to the much fruit He was to bear through His death.

Here Paul interjects the exclamation, "by grace have ye been saved," to give direct expression to his readers of what is implied in his words, viz. that this work of God includes real and complete salvation, and that that is entirely of His free, unbought, and undeserved favour. This was the characteristic point of the gospel that Paul preached, and he resumes and

6 saved;) and hath raised *us* up together, and made *us* sit
7 together in heavenly *places* in Christ Jesus: that in the

expands the thought in vers. 8–10. Meanwhile, after the ejaculation that has burst out from his full heart, he continues his description of how God makes us partakers with Christ in that train of events in which His power and His love are shown in His exaltation from the depths of earth to the heights of heaven.

6. **and raised us up with him, and made us to sit with him in the heavenly** *places*, **in Christ Jesus:**] The raising up, as distinguished from the quickening, is the calling into exercise of the life that is implanted by the former act. When Jesus called Lazarus out of his sepulchre, we must conceive of a mysterious act of divine power reanimating the dead clay before the ears could hear, or the limbs obey, the voice that cried, "Lazarus, come forth." So in the description of the resurrection of the two witnesses in the vision (Rev. xi. 11), it is said "the breath of life from God entered into them," that corresponds to our being quickened with Christ; "and they stood upon their feet," that corresponds to our being raised up with Christ. There is no interval of time between the two acts, but there is a distinction in the order of nature; and there is the difference, that the first must be conceived as purely an act of God, without any co-operation of those who are quickened; while in the second, the powers of the life thus imparted are exerted, in obedience to the call of God, and by the co-operation of His sustaining power. The distinction is of no importance in the case of physical resurrection, hence Paul did not notice it in his description of the exaltation of Christ (ch. i. 20); but it is important in our spiritual resurrection, as showing that, while this is due to God's mighty power, and we cannot be conceived as co-operating with Him in giving ourselves life, yet from the moment that life is given, we are and must be active in the exercise of it. This explains and justifies the statement in the Westminster Confession, ch. x. § 2: "This effectual call is of God's free and special grace alone, not from anything at all foreseen in man; who is altogether passive therein, until, being quickened and renewed by the Holy Spirit, he is thereby enabled to answer this call and to embrace the grace offered and conveyed in it." Observe that the grace is not only offered, but conveyed, in the call by which we are raised from our death in sin. It is as when Christ said to the paralytic, "Rise, take up thy bed, and walk." He had no power to do so; and though he could have no part in giving himself the power, yet at once, on the call coming, he received and exerted the power. The need of an act of divine power, to enable us to turn from sin to God, should not therefore hinder any from complying with the call to repentance and faith, which is freely addressed to all.

But our fellowship with Christ in His exaltation extends also to the further stage of it, "he made us to sit with him in the heavenlies." Even this may be understood as a present privilege, of real practical value. Our former state the apostle had described (ver. 2) as a walking after the prince of the power of the air; but now he says we are raised above that, into the heavenlies," *i.e.* we are freed from the dominion of those powers of evil by which we were led away captive before. So Jesus said, "I beheld Satan fallen as lightning from heaven. Behold, I have given you power to tread upon serpents and scorpions, and over all the power of the enemy" (Luke x. 18, 19). His being seated in the heavenlies implies His being raised above all principality and power; and our being seated there with Him is seen in our being raised above these powers of evil, with their prince,

ages to come he might show the exceeding riches of his grace in *his* kindness towards us through Christ Jesus. 8 For by grace are ye saved through faith; and that not of 9 yourselves: *it is* the gift of God: not of works, lest any man

whose realm, though above the earth, is only the lower aerial, not the celestial region. It has been noticed that Paul does not say of us, as he does of Christ, that God has seated us at His right hand. That is the peculiar prerogative of the Son of God, who is head over all things to His Church; but we are raised to the same region of rest and victory over the spiritual foes that once enslaved us.

7. **that in the ages to come he might shew the exceeding riches of his grace in kindness toward us in Christ Jesus:**] The purpose of this wonderful work of salvation does not terminate with us, but looks far beyond. Paul sees in the future a long vista of ages coming on, one behind another, in every one of which God designs that His grace should be known, as passing all bounds in its riches: and His kindness towards us in Christ is so marvellous, lifting us from such a depth, and exalting us to such a height, through such a Saviour, that it is fitted to be an exhibition to all ages, and to all ranks of God's intelligent creatures, of the vastness of grace that is in Him. This great end may in some measure explain why God was pleased to allow a portion, possibly only a very small part in relation to the whole of His rational creatures, to fall into such awful ruin, since by their gracious deliverance from it, the riches of His grace is made known to countless generations of beings yet uncreated, so as to draw forth their love, and secure their loyalty and free obedience to the God of love. The introduction of this idea not only serves to elevate and expand our thoughts of God's greatness and goodness, but also to humble our pride. "Not for your sakes do I this," said God to Israel, "but for my holy name's sake." We must never let the greatness of what God does for us make us proud that we are specially valuable in His eyes. He has indeed, as before said, a real pity and love for us personally; but it is for His own sake, that the riches of His grace may be made known, that He saves us with such a salvation.

8, 9. **for by grace have ye been saved through faith; and that not of yourselves: *it is* the gift of God: not of works, that no man should glory.**] In confirmation of the thought of ver. 7, Paul repeats and amplifies the statement he had introduced as an ejaculation (ver. 5), that salvation is due entirely to God's grace, *i.e.* His free, undeserved, unbought favour. Here, as before, he speaks of salvation as an accomplished fact, while elsewhere his more common expression describes it as a process that is still going on, and called, "those who are being saved." That brings out the truth that our deliverance from sin and its consequences is a gradual work, which must be constantly proceeding, all through our life in this world. But the process begins by a radical change, which virtually accomplishes and secures its completion in due time, and that is the point which it was suitable to emphasise here; since the power and the love of God, displayed in our conversion, are the theme on which the apostle has been speaking.

That which answers to grace on God's part, is faith on ours; and Paul here sums up in a sentence what he had expounded at length in Rom. iv. and Gal. iii.: thus showing that, though in this and his other later epistles he introduces new thoughts and points of view, he has not forgotten, nor become

10 should boast. For we are his workmanship, created in Christ Jesus unto good works, which God hath before ordained

indifferent to, those for which he so earnestly pleaded against the Judaising party whom he had to oppose at an earlier time.

Whether the following clause, "and that not of yourselves," refers to faith, or to "ye have been saved," is a doubtful question ; for both interpretations are grammatically possible, and, while the ancient commentators generally understood it of faith, the majority of modern interpreters, including Calvin, refer it to salvation. The chief reason for this latter opinion is that the following clause (ver. 9), "not of works," can hardly be connected with faith, but must refer to salvation. But it is quite in Paul's style to interrupt the direct connection of his thoughts by a parenthetic clause such as this, so that the construction would be : " by grace ye have been saved through faith . . . not of works " ; while the words, " and that not of yourselves, God's is the gift," come in as a parenthesis. In favour of this, it has been observed that the words "and that," always in Paul's writings, indicate some addition to a preceding assertion ; and further, that if the reference is only to salvation, there would be an extraordinary repetition of the same thought in three or four ways : "ye are saved by grace, your salvation is not of yourselves, it is God's gift, not of works"; whereas, if the reference is to faith, each clause adds something to the thought ; and there are just two distinct antitheses, "ye are saved by grace through faith ; not of works ; and your faith is not of your own originating, but the gift of God." Paul admittedly teaches this about faith elsewhere ; and it seems the most natural construction of his words here, although there is no doctrinal issue involved in the decision. In any view, the passage is a remarkably strong expression of the absolute freeness of salvation. Faith indeed is required on our part, for God will not save us against our will, or do any violence to the freedom of choice that is essential to responsibility ; but faith is simply our receiving God's salvation in Christ, and is opposed to all works : and this way of salvation has been chosen by God, in order that none may have any ground of boasting, as if he had received God's grace on account of any merit or goodness of his own. Compare for the thought, Rom. iii. 27, 28, iv. 14–16.

10. **For we are his workmanship, created in Christ Jesus for good works, which God afore prepared that we should walk in them.**] So far from our being able to obtain salvation by our works, we are ourselves the work of God, made by Him, not only as we owe our being to His creative power, but as we owe our new life, and our power for any really good works, to His newcreating energy. That divine agency, the mighty power of which Paul desired his readers to know, which he had just described as a quickening and raising from death, he designates here as a making or creating, thus illustrating it by the analogy of not one only, but all the greatest acts of God's power.

But even in this most emphatic assertion of our salvation by the free grace of God, Paul shows, as always, his earnest concern for moral interests, which might seem to be endangered by such a doctrine. While absolutely denying that we are saved *by* good works, he asserts with equal strength that we are saved *for* good works ; and thus refusing to allow morality to be the means, gives it the higher place of the end, of salvation. We are created in Christ unto good works, and that too not as a sort of afterthought, or mere secondary result, but as the object contemplated by God from the beginning. As he had said before, that God chose us in Christ before the foundation of

11 that we should walk in them. Wherefore remember, that ye *being* in time past Gentiles in the flesh, who are called Uncircumcision by that which is called the Circumcision in the
12 flesh made by hands; that at that time ye were without Christ, being aliens from the commonwealth of Israel, and

the world that we should be holy and without blemish, so he says here, that God afore prepared the good works for which we are created in Christ. He has provided in the constitution of the world means and opportunities for His children exercising goodness, kindness, love, after the pattern of His own, in the activities of a new life. The form of expression here reminds us of Jesus' parable of the master of the house appointing his servants to each one his work (Mark xiii. 34), and giving them talents according to their ability (Matt. xxv. 16). Thus God has prepared for each of us a task to be done for Him, a part to be occupied, a talent to be employed; and our walking in the faithful discharge of these duties has the supreme importance assigned to it, of being the end to which all His wonderful work in our redemption, calling, and new creation is but the means.

II. 11-22. *Reminder of their changed Position.*—On the ground of their great spiritual change, Paul calls upon his readers to remember the position in which they had once been, as Gentiles. The change from death to life, which he has been describing, is common to all Christians; for he had said, we Jews were by nature children of wrath, even as the rest. But Gentiles were in a condition of peculiar alienation, and they ought to know and remember that from this also they are saved by Christ.

11. Wherefore remember, that aforetime ye, the Gentiles in the flesh, who are called Uncircumcision by that which is called Circumcision, in the flesh, made by hands;] The word "aforetime" (A. V., "in time past") should come, according to the best authorities, not after but before "ye." The meaning is not that they were once Gentiles but are so now no longer, for that was not the case. In so far as the name denoted a distinction of race, it belonged to them still; and the reason of adding the words "in the flesh" would seem to be just to show that it was so meant. By birth they were of the nations outside of God's people Israel; and they had not received the mark of circumcision, by which some proselytes had been incorporated into the Jewish Church and nation. Hence they were called contemptuously "Uncircumcised" by those who proudly called themselves "the Circumcision," *i.e.* sealed as God's people, although their circumcision was but the outward cutting of the flesh by human hands, not the real putting off the sins of the flesh, which alone truly makes men God's people. Paul made this distinction between ritual and spiritual circumcision in Rom. ii. 25-29; and in Phil. iii. 1-3, he gives the Jewish formalists the name "Concision," mere cutting; while he claims for spiritual worshippers the honourable name of "Circumcision," the seal of God's covenant. The same thought seems to have been in his mind here, but he gives it only passing expression. For his main purpose is to remind them that though the ritual and external differences that still subsist between them and the Jews are not essential, yet in their former state as heathens they had really been further from God than those who had received the revelation of His promise. Accordingly the next verse resumes and completes the sentence.

12. that ye were at that time separate from Christ, alienated from the

strangers from the covenants of promise, having no hope,
13 and without God in the world : but now, in Christ Jesus, ye

commonwealth of Israel, and strangers from the covenants of the promise, having no hope and without God in the world.] This is what he would have them remember. At that time, before they heard and believed the gospel, their separation from Israel implied more than a mere outward and nominal difference. They were really alienated from God, and therefore in a very sad and dark condition; while there was a community that enjoyed His presence and promise. The description of this destitute state begins with an expression that may at first surprise us, "separate from Christ." For it may be said, were not all men alike in that state before Christ came? It is not to be weakened down to the meaning, without the promise or expectation of the Messiah; but is rather to be understood by contrast with what Paul had said before and repeats emphatically in the following verse, that now they are in Christ. It represents Christ, however, as really existing, and in some sense in fellowship with men, before He came in the flesh ; and this is in accordance with Paul's statements elsewhere. In 1 Cor. x. 4, and perhaps 9, he speaks of Christ as present with the Israelites in their wilderness journey; and though he may have conceived of that as only an ideal or figurative presence, in Phil. ii. 5-7 he ascribes to Christ Jesus acts of thought and will before He appeared as a man. We need not, therefore, hesitate to give the words here their natural sense, that the Gentiles were destitute of a relation to Christ, which believing Israelites had. Having said this, Paul goes on to indicate first the causes, and then the consequences of it. Its causes are declared in the clauses, "being alienated from the commonwealth of Israel, and strangers from the covenants of the promise." There was a people in the world who were not all separate from Christ, but were united to God by covenants, which contained a promise of blessing to them, and to all the families of the earth. Referring to them, Paul uses the God-given name Israel, not the mere human and external designation "the circumcision," which he had employed before, indicating that those who were Israelites indeed had real and precious blessings, from which the Gentiles were alienated. The form of the participle cannot be pressed to indicate that they had been separated from a community to which they once belonged ; for that is not a historical fact, and Paul could not have meant to assert it. There is only emphasised the completeness of the separation. The commonwealth of Israel belonged to others, not to them ; such is the literal force of the word. The following clause shows what is implied in this, that they were also strangers from the covenants of the promise. The great distinction of Israel was to be in covenant with God, as Paul said elsewhere (Rom. ix. 4); and in both places he speaks of the covenants in the plural, referring to the various occasions on which God renewed His gracious engagements to the patriarchs and to the people. He calls them here covenants of the promise, that is, the great promise of God's mercy and blessing which was summed up in the words so often repeated, to be a God unto them. From these covenants the Gentiles had been strangers ; if any had an interest in them, it could only be as guests within the gates of God's people.

The consequences of this alienation are next described. As thus strangers to the covenants of the promise, they had no hope, that is, no certain or confident hope ; for that can only be built on a word of God. We need not suppose that the apostle means to deny absolutely to the Gentiles any hope,

who sometimes were far off are made nigh by the blood of in the wide sense of a vague idea of the possibility of mercy from God, such as the Ninevites are described as expressing, "Who knoweth whether God will not turn and repent, and turn from his fierce anger, that we perish not?" (Jonah iii. 9). But they had not the sure hope that God by His revelation of promise had enabled Israel to cherish. And as the climax of their sad condition, they are described as having been "without God in the world." They were not, indeed, entirely ignorant of God; for Paul teaches elsewhere (Rom. i. 19, 20, ii. 14, 15), they had a knowledge of God and His law, from the works of nature and the testimony of their own consciences. But they had not retained God in their knowledge; they had been worshipping beings, real or imaginary, which are not God; and their polytheism was, as the Christians called it, atheistic; they had no intercourse or fellowship with the true God, and were living as if He were not. They were not in the kingdom of God, the commonwealth of Israel, but in the world, which in its wisdom knew not God.

This dark picture is but too true a likeness of the general state of the heathen world before Christ came, and even now where the gospel has not been received; and it is well fitted to awaken our pity, and our prayers and efforts towards its enlightenment and conversion to God. But it need not be pressed so far as to imply, that every single person in these nations is absolutely estranged from God. Even in the darkest night of ignorance, He has never left Himself without witness; and in every nation he that feareth Him and worketh righteousness is acceptable to Him.

> "We grant 'tis true that heaven from mortal sense
> Hath hid the secret paths of Providence;
> Yet boundless wisdom, boundless goodness, may
> Find even for those bewildered souls a way;
> And though no name be for salvation known
> But that of God's eternal Son alone,
> Who knows how far transcending mercy can
> Extend the merits of that Son to man."

But the apostle's present object is to show by contrast the riches of God's grace in the conversion of the Gentiles.

13. **But now in Christ Jesus ye that once were far off are made nigh in the blood of Christ.**] Thus briefly and emphatically is the great change described. "In Christ Jesus" is now their condition, contrasted with their former one, "separate from Christ"; and the definite, personal name Jesus is added to show that it is not merely an ideal or promised Messiah, but the actual historical Saviour in whom they now are. The relation expressed by "in" is the same as that described in ch. i. 3-14. Being thus in Christ, ye, who before ye believed in Him were, as before described, afar off from God, have been made nigh; and that "in the blood of Christ." This is not a mere repetition and enlargement of the phrase "in Christ Jesus," but adds a statement of the special way in which we are brought nigh. The blood refers to Christ's death on the cross, as in ch. i. 7; and the preposition "in" is nearly equivalent to "through" there, but possibly it is chosen because in the phraseology used about the priests drawing near to God in the temple, the expression literally is "he shall come in a young bullock, for a sin-offering," etc. (Lev. xvi. 3). This idiom is preserved in the Greek translation, though not in the English; and in Heb. ix. 25 we read, "the high priest enters into the holiest in the blood of others"; and ch. x. 19, "we have

14 Christ. For he is our peace, who hath made both one, and hath broken down the middle wall of partition *between*
15 *us*; having abolished in his flesh the enmity, *even* the law of commandments *contained* in ordinances; for to make in him-

boldness to enter into the holiest in the blood of Jesus." How Christ's death is the way of our being brought nigh is explained in what follows.

14, 15a. For he is our peace, who made both one, and brake down the middle wall of partition, having abolished in his flesh the enmity, *even* the law of commandments *contained* in ordinances;] The explanation is, that He is our peace, literally He Himself, for the pronoun is emphatic. He is not only our peace-maker, but Himself our peace; because we enjoy the peace that He brings no otherwise than by being in Him; and He proved Himself to be this, by making both Israel and the Gentiles one, not, as is shown afterward, by merely uniting the Gentiles to Israel, but by making both into a higher unity in the Christian Church. That this is so, is shown by the following clauses, which describe further what Christ has done. He "brake down the middle wall of partition," or rather "of the fence"; for the word is definite, and does not convey the idea of separation, which is only contained in the expression "middle wall," but that of enclosure. The ancient interpreters refer appositely to Isaiah's parable of the vineyard of the Lord, of which it is said that He had made a trench or a hedge about it (Isa. v. 2, 5). The law given to Israel was a fence about them, intended for their protection and safety; but when they transgressed, it became a hedge separating between them and God. Paul may have had in his mind the stone fence in the temple area, beyond which no uncircumcised person was allowed to pass on pain of death, and of which a stone bearing an inscription to that effect was found not long ago. But he merely alludes to it; and what he properly means is, not so much what separated Gentiles from Jews, but what separated them both from God.

The words "the enmity," which in the original come immediately after "the middle wall of the fence," may be governed either by the verb that precedes, "brake down," or by that which follows, "having abolished." The translators and revisers of the English Bible have preferred the latter construction; but the clause might equally well be rendered thus, "who brake down the middle wall of the fence, the enmity, in his flesh, having abolished the law of commandments in ordinances." This seems on the whole more natural. The figurative expression, "middle wall of the fence," seems to need an explanation, which is given by the words "the enmity"; and the clause "in his flesh" tells how Christ has broken down this. The enmity is that which separated men from God, the law pronouncing its curse against all transgressors. Christ has taken that out of the way in His flesh, *i.e.* in His body as nailed to the cross, by which He became a curse for us, and so bought us out from the curse of the law (Gal. iii. 13). In doing this, He has abolished, *i.e.* made powerless, the law of commandments in ordinances. The insertion of the word "contained" is somewhat doubtful; and the words "in ordinances" may be connected with having abolished, "in respect of ordinances," *i.e.* as prescribing conditions of acceptance with God.

Some would understand by the law of commandments here merely the ceremonial statutes; but it is more in harmony with the natural meaning, and with Paul's general teaching, to understand it of the whole law, though

16 self of twain one new man, *so* making peace; and that he might reconcile both unto God in one body by the cross, 17 having slain the enmity thereby; and came and preached peace to you which were afar off, and to them that were nigh.

only in one particular aspect of it, that of ordinances under which men are held in bondage. In its principles and spirit, as revealing God's character and will, believers, according to Paul, are still to obey it.

15*b*, 16. that he might create in himself of the twain one new man, *so* making peace; and might reconcile them both in one body unto God through the cross, having slain the enmity thereby:] These clauses express the purpose of the work of Christ just mentioned; and describe it as twofold, in reference to the double enmity before spoken of, that between Jews and Gentiles, and that between them both and God. The former is thoroughly removed only when the latter is also: for men can be really united to one another only when they are all united to God. Christ's purpose in annulling the law in ordinances was not merely to incorporate the Gentiles in the commonwealth of Israel, but to create them both into a new community, one new man, as Paul puts it, in a vivid figure. This He does "in himself." He is really the second Man, in whom the human race is made a harmonious unity, and all things are to be summed up as their head. Thus He makes peace where there had been division and discord. But His purpose is also to reconcile them both to God, that is, according to the usage of the expression, both in general and with Paul in particular, to remove not merely their opposition to God, but God's displeasure against them. It is, indeed, worthy of notice that the Bible never speaks of Christ reconciling God to us, but only of His reconciling us to God, or God reconciling us to Himself, so as to exclude all idea of God being unwilling to forgive us, or being persuaded by Christ to do so. Yet it is clear that the barrier between us and God was something more than our enmity against Him. There was also His holy anger against sin. So the reconcilation to God effected by Christ is said to be through the cross; and by a bold figure it is added, "having slain the enmity thereby." By dying He put to death that which killed Him; he annulled the law of commandments in ordinances; and also, by the constraining influence of the love manifested in His self-sacrifice, He melts the hearts of sinners, and turns them to God. He reconciles them "in one body." This has been understood, by some, of Christ's natural body; by others, of the Church which is His body: but probably both are meant here. Those who are reconciled to God must be in Christ, in vital union with the Saviour, who still possesses His human body, now exalted and glorified; and, as thus in His body, they constitute the one spiritual body, of which He is the head, and in which all enmity and division is done away, and peace reigns.

17. **and he came and preached good tidings of peace to you that were far off, and peace to them that were nigh:**] Paul has shown how Christ is our peace (ver. 14), and how He has made peace (ver. 15); now he goes on to describe how he proclaimed the glad tidings of peace. The words "he came" (literally, "having come") are by some referred to His coming into the world by His incarnation. But there are two weighty objections to this. (1) After having spoken of His death on the cross, it would be unnatural to go back to what was earlier, in a clause that evidently continues the account

18 For through him we both have access by one Spirit unto the
19 Father. Now therefore ye are no more strangers and foreigners, but fellow-citizens with the saints, and of the household

of what Christ has done for us. (2) It cannot be said that in His earthly life, when He said He was not sent but to the lost sheep of the house of Israel, He preached peace to the Gentiles that were afar. It is better, therefore, to understand it of His coming after His resurrection, when He appeared to His disciples with the greeting, "Peace be unto you," and sent them to make disciples of all nations, and proclaim the glad tidings to every creature. Through them, by His word and Spirit, He comes in all the world, bringing glad tidings of peace to all alike, the Gentiles who were afar off, and the Jews who were near, both alike needed to be reconciled to God. The words Paul uses are taken from Isa. lvii. 19, where the prophet, after having in ch. lvi. given promises of grace to the strangers who joined themselves to the Lord, and shown the guilt of the ungodly Israelites, proclaims God's mercy to both alike, on the common ground of human frailty and sin. Thus the apostle would indicate that the great blessing of New Testament times, of which he was the herald, had been foreshadowed of old by the prophets.

18. **for through him we both have our access in one Spirit unto the Father.**] This clause shows how true it is that Christ brings glad news of peace, both to those that are far off and to those that are near, since it is through Him that both alike have their access to God, who is here designated "the Father," to indicate the nearness and lovingness of the relation to Him into which Christ brings us. This is truly peace with God, when we can draw near to Him as our Father; and since Jew and Gentile alike have this privilege through Christ, because it is He who has taken away the barrier interposed by the law in ordinances, these must be at peace among themselves. All the more, because they have this access in one Spirit. Before (ver. 16), Paul had said they were reconciled "in one body," *i.e.* not as two separate communities, but a single higher one including both: now he adds "in one Spirit," to show that the unity is not a mere outward one, but implies a oneness of heart and will, wrought by the one Spirit of God by whom they are all sealed.

19. **So then ye are no more strangers and sojourners, but ye are fellow-citizens with the saints, and of the household of God,**] Here he draws the conclusion from the whole description of the work of Christ (vers. 13–18). Ye are no more strangers, as ye were before (ver. 12), *i.e.* outside the kingdom of God entirely; nor even sojourners, that is, resident foreigners, such as were found in most ancient States, enjoying some measure of protection and privilege, but not the full rights of citizens. Such was the position of proselytes in Israel. But now Paul says to his Gentile readers, ye are no longer in any inferior position, but fellow-citizens with the saints, *i.e.* the people whom God has separated to Himself out of the world. Ye have all the privileges which these enjoy; nay, ye have them in common with them, so that there is absolutely no difference, since all alike now have these privileges on the same ground, that of the reconciling work of Christ. Yea, ye have, through Him, an even more blessed position than the saints under the old covenant had, ye are "of the household of God," not merely citizens of the kingdom of God, but children of His family. This flows from the access to God as Father asserted in ver. 18.

20 of God; and are built upon the foundation of the apostles
and prophets, Jesus Christ himself being the chief corner
21 *stone*; in whom all the building, fitly framed together, groweth

20. **being built upon the foundation of the apostles and prophets, Christ Jesus himself being the chief corner stone;**] The figure is here changed from the household to the material house; and though, in one point of view, it seems a lower thing to be stones in a building than children in a family, yet it expresses vividly the idea of permanence and stability in their position, which is an additional and very precious privilege (comp. Rev. iii. 12). The Gentile believers are described as having been built up on a foundation, which is described as that of the apostles and prophets; while Christ Jesus Himself is said to be the chief corner stone. By the prophets here some have understood those of the O. T.; but since, in two later places of this epistle, prophets are mentioned along with apostles as Christian office-bearers (chs. iii. 5, iv. 11), we must understand the name here also in the same sense, as denoting those who in the early Church received direct communications from God for the guidance of the believers (see Acts xi. 27, xiii. 1; 1 Cor. xiv.). But what is meant by the foundation of the apostles and prophets? Grammatically, the words may mean either (*a*) the foundation which consists of them, or (*b*) laid by them, or (*c*) on which they rest; and each of these constructions has found supporters. The ground of decision must lie chiefly in the form of the image here used. In the original passage, from which the various uses of this figure are derived (Isa. xxviii. 16, expressly quoted in 1 Pet. ii. 6), the foundation and the corner stone are the same, and both names are applied to Christ. Here, however, the two are distinguished; and, while Christ is called the corner stone, the foundation is spoken of separately. This seems to make the third explanation (*c*) above mentioned impossible, for that on which the apostles and prophets rest could only be Christ, and the distinct mention of Him as the corner stone would be unmeaning. To hold, as some do, that it is the doctrine or testimony of the apostles and prophets, is unnatural, because it has been already said that Christ Himself proclaimed peace (ver. 17). Besides, the Church is never represented as founded upon a doctrine or testimony, but always on the person of Christ. Those, however, who have been united to Christ in genuine faith are sometimes represented as forming part of the foundation (1 Cor. iii. 10–17; 2 Tim. ii. 19; Matt. xvi. 18); and this seems to be the meaning here. This is compatible with either the first (*a*) or the second (*b*) of the possible constructions; but it seems more agreeable to Paul's mode of speaking elsewhere to understand it as the foundation laid by the apostles and prophets, *i.e.* those who by their ministry had been built on Christ. When the Gentiles were called, there were already many such, forming the foundation of God (2 Tim. ii. 19), to whom they were added; and so this clause is parallel to "fellow-citizens with the saints" (ver. 19). But these are not the ultimate ground of confidence. The foundation would not be secure unless it were bound at the corner by one great and immovable stone, to which all the others were joined; and so Christ Jesus is declared to be the chief corner stone, the one at the very point of the angle, belonging equally to both walls and binding both together, as well as sustaining the weight of the whole building.

21. **in whom each several building** (*Gr.* every building; A. V. all the building), **fitly framed together, groweth into a holy temple in**

22 unto an holy temple in the Lord : in whom ye also are builded together for an habitation of God through the Spirit.

CHAP. III. 1. For this cause, I Paul, the prisoner of Jesus Christ

the Lord ;] The Revisers have here given the strictly grammatical meaning of the best attested text ; but it is not certain that the less exact idiom, by which "all building" was used for "all the building," may not have been employed by Paul, nor that the words, strictly construed, would convey the meaning of various different structures forming part of one great temple. We cannot lay much stress upon the absence of the definite article as pointing to the freedom and mutual independence of each part of the Church, while built on one common foundation. But we should emphasise the fact that the building is described as not complete and finished, but gradually going on. Each part is being fitted in to another, and all are in Christ, the corner stone bounds and determines the form of the entire building, and as stone after stone is built in, the edifice grows apace. Nor is this a mere common or ordinary building : it is to be a temple, consecrated to the Lord. But it can be that only "in the Lord," *i.e.* the Lord Jesus. This clause can hardly be connected with "groweth" ; for the growth has already been said to be in Christ Jesus, the corner stone. But as the relations of Christ to believers are far too intimate and comprehensive to be expressed by any one figure, especially by one so external as that of the corner stone ; it is added that only in the Lord can believers become a holy temple. He is Himself the true temple ; and it is only as we are in Him by faith that we can form any part of that wonderful and glorious edifice.

22. **in whom ye also are builded together for** (*Gr.* unto) **a habitation of God in the Spirit.**] Once more, in the final clause of this wonderful paragraph, the apostle addresses directly his Gentile readers, and assures them that they also, as well as the believing Jews, are being built up in Christ, along with all the other saints, in the great temple of which he is at once the corner stone and the surrounding presence and glory. In doing so, He exalts the image to the very highest point of dignity. He had described it as a building surely founded, well compacted, a temple for the worship of God ; but now he adds that the temple is not only consecrated to, but inhabited by, God. It is so in the Spirit, which is the truest and best way in which God can reveal His presence ; for He who manifested Himself on earth in the person of Jesus of Nazareth, now comes in the Spirit, whom Jesus, after He was glorified, sent from heaven. The Spirit of God dwells in all and each of those who are truly Christ's, and by the Spirit the Father and the Son come and make their abode with them.

III. 1-21. *Appeal as the prisoner of Christ for the Gentiles.*

III. 1. **For this cause I Paul, the prisoner of Christ Jesus in behalf of you Gentiles,**] The sentence thus begun must be regarded as broken off at the end of the verse ; for the attempts that many good expositors have made to complete it, by supplying a verb, are forbidden by insuperable difficulties. Such interruptions are not infrequent in Paul's writings, and there has been one already in this epistle (ch. ii. 1-4). That and similar passages in other epistles show, that the things that break the grammatical connection of his sentences are not always subordinate ideas, or parenthetic digressions, but often contribute important or necessary links in the main line of thought.

This peculiarity of style is not due to a loose and rambling habit of thought, but to a haste in the utterance of a remarkable fulness of ideas that will not suffer him to take time to put them in a smooth and orderly connection. As with the style of Thucydides and of Cromwell, with which Paul's has been aptly compared, the abundance of matter often wrecks the grammar ; and we have to regard the connection of the thoughts rather than of the words.

There have been several views as to where the apostle resumes the thought he had begun to express in this verse. Some have found it at ver. 8, some at ver. 13, and the greater number of modern interpreters think that at ver. 14, where he repeats the opening words of ver. 1, "for this cause," he takes up again what he had meant to say. Thus it is thought, that Paul intended to follow up what he had said of the blessed privileges of the Gentile believers by a prayer for them ; but is so filled with the subject of his own relation to God's great purpose for mankind, that he delays his prayer for a few moments to express this. But is this natural? Would Paul, if intending simply to offer a prayer for his readers, put forward his own person and condition so prominently as he does in ver. 1? In all the various instances in which he does so elsewhere (Gal. v. 2; Rom. xi. 13; 2 Cor. x. 1; Philem. 9), it is for the purpose of enforcing some truth or duty which might need his authority and influence to prevail with those addressed. Again, how is the conditional clause in ver. 2 to be explained, "if so be ye have heard"? Did either Paul's purpose to pray for them, or the fact of his being the prisoner of Christ for them, depend on their knowledge of this? It seems far more natural to suppose that Paul is about to address to his readers those lofty exhortations to Christian duty that are contained in chs. iv.–vi. : and that, in order that they might be effectual, he presents himself to them, not only as the apostle of Christ to the Gentiles, but as one who was even then suffering bonds on their behalf. The force of this appeal would plainly depend on their knowing the truth of this; and so he is naturally led to refresh their memories in regard to it, and to show what it involved. The inferential conjunctions in vers. 13 and 14 can, as we shall see, be explained quite naturally as founded on what immediately precedes them. I think, therefore, that the view of the connection given in the Authorised Version is the best, that the sentence here begun is not resumed and completed till ch. iv. 1, when Paul repeats, not indeed the very words with which he began, but the main idea, "the prisoner of the Lord." The objection which has deterred most recent expositors from adopting it, is that the chapter is too long and important to be a parenthesis or digression. But the only way in which we can avoid making the larger part of the chapter apparently such, is the admittedly untenable one of making ver. 1 a complete sentence. And the parenthesis is only seeming, for what interrupts the construction is a necessary explanation and support of the first clause.

"For this cause," *i.e.* on account of the great blessings and precious privileges that the Gentile believers had received, as he had just been reminding them (ch. ii. 13–22), Paul now addresses them with a more pointed assertion of his own person and condition than he had made before. "I Paul, the prisoner of Christ Jesus," *i.e.* who am in confinement, wearing a chain that fastens me to a soldier of the Roman army, for Christ's sake and at His command, and that more especially in behalf of you Gentiles," since it was on account of his preaching the kingdom of God to the Gentiles, and maintaining their right to a position in it equally with the Israelites, that Paul had been persecuted by the Jews, and through their murderous hate made a

2 for you Gentiles, (if ye have heard of the dispensation of the
3 grace of God which is given me to you-ward: how that by
revelation he made known unto me the mystery; as I wrote
4 afore in few words; whereby, when ye read, ye may under-
5 stand my knowledge in the mystery of Christ; which in

prisoner by the Roman authorities. Such was actually his position when he wrote, and he would have his words received by his Gentile readers with the attention due to a man who had laboured and suffered, and was still suffering, in order that the blessing he has just described might be theirs. He suggests this to them with a noble simplicity in these few words.

2. **if so be that ye have heard of the dispensation of that grace of God which was given me to you-ward;]** This is the necessary supposition of his address, and he does not go on to follow it up till he has made sure that it is understood. "If so be" does not necessarily imply doubt; but it is extremely unlikely that Paul would have written so, and gone on to explain so fully his calling and mission, if he were writing only to those who, like the Ephesian believers, were familiarly acquainted with him by a ministry of three years among them. It is more probable that he has in view some, at least, who, though they had received the gospel, had not been made aware of the part that Paul had been called to take in its proclamation. In Asia, as in other places, there were professing Christians who were opposed to Paul, and ashamed of his chain.

By changing "the grace" into "that grace," the Revisers have shown, what is plain in the original, that the clause "which was given" refers not to dispensation, but to the grace of God. Hence dispensation cannot here mean stewardship, as an office bestowed on Paul; but must denote the way and manner in which God bestows the gifts of His grace. God is thus conceived as a great and wise householder, dispensing His stores of blessing, so as best to make them available for the many who are to receive them. He bestows special favours on some, in order that through them blessings may be conveyed to many others. By the grace, which Paul says was given to him, we need not understand anything else than that revelation of God's Son in him, of which he tells the Galatians that it was in order that he might preach Him to the Gentiles (Gal. i. 16). He never distinguishes his own personal forgiveness, his being shown God's universal grace, and his mission to the heathen: all three virtually came to him at once, when he recognised the crucified Jesus as the Messiah. So the grace of personal reconciliation to God was given him toward the Gentiles, with a view to their conversion and blessing. But the element of revelation is most prominent here.

3. **how that by revelation was made known unto me the mystery, as I wrote afore in few words,]** "Mystery," as before explained, means simply secret, something that cannot be discovered by the unaided search of men, but must be unveiled by God; though, when unveiled, it may not be mysterious in the modern sense. What is the secret here meant is stated in ver. 6; and when Paul says, "I wrote afore," he refers, not to any former epistle, but to the earlier part of this one, especially ch. i. 9, 10, where in few words is stated the universal grace and saving purpose of God.

4. **whereby, when ye read, ye can perceive my understanding in the mystery of Christ;]** This is not a boastful statement, as on a hasty perusal it is apt to appear. On the contrary, it shows that the apostle does not stand

other ages was not made known unto the sons of men, as it is now revealed unto his holy apostles and prophets by the

on his mere personal authority, and ask them to believe simply because he has received a revelation, and declares it to them. He tells them they can judge for themselves, as they read what he has written. The secret when disclosed is seen to be worthy of God and of Christ; and though they could not have ventured to anticipate such wonderful grace and love on the part of God, yet, when it is declared to them, they can see and feel that it is Godlike, and that Paul cannot have invented or dreamed it, but must have rightly understood the mystery of Christ. Here, as always in the New Testament, all men, even the ignorant and unlearned, are invited to read and search the Scriptures for themselves; and are assured that, if they do so, they will see in itself sufficient evidence of its divine origin and truth. The word "read" has been supposed to refer to reading aloud, as it usually does in the New Testament; but since it is said of the Christians in general, to whom Paul is writing, and not merely of their ministers, it cannot be limited to that.

The mystery or secret of the Christ may denote that which pertains to him as its subject; but as Paul, in the parallel epistle to the Colossians (ch. i. 27), speaks of Christ Himself as the mystery, his meaning may be the same here; and we have already observed (on ver. 2) that the revelation by which the mystery was unveiled to Paul was by God revealing His Son in him.

5. which in other generations was not made known unto the sons of men, as it hath now been revealed unto his holy apostles and prophets in the Spirit;] This clause, too, is a modest rather than an arrogant statement, as the epithet "holy" given to the apostles, of whom he was one, has led some to think. For its scope is to show that the revelation of the great secret was not made to Paul alone, though he was the apostle of the Gentiles, but was now disclosed to all the inspired teachers of the Church, because the time had come, in God's ordering of the world's history, when it was fitting that it should be so revealed. There is a studied contrast between the two clauses of the verse, which explains the use of the word "holy" here. The former clause describes the incapacity of human nature: hence the Old Testament phrase "sons of men," here only used by Paul, and, especially along with "in other generations," suggesting the idea of human birth, and that they who are only born of the flesh cannot see the kingdom of God. Then the expression "was not made known" in its generality, covering all kinds and ways of knowledge, is contrasted with "has been revealed," to denote the special way of divine illumination. This is granted to apostles and prophets, not simply as sons of men, but as Christ's holy ones, *i.e.* men who belong to Him, who are no longer their own but His. The word is not used in the superstitious sense of later ecclesiastical language, for it is applied, both before and after in this epistle, to all Christians alike; and apostles and prophets are twice mentioned without this or any epithet, so that it is plain that it is introduced here to convey the important idea that God's revelation is made to those who are His loyal people. "The secret of the Lord is with them that fear him." The contrast with the mere human powers indicated in the former clause is finally heightened by the words, "in the Spirit," *i.e.* the Spirit of God, showing how the revelation is conveyed to their minds. We can hardly lay great stress on the word "as," so that it should indicate

6 Spirit; that the Gentiles should be fellow-heirs, and of the same body, and partakers of his promise in Christ by the
7 gospel: whereof I was made a minister, according to the gift of the grace of God given unto me by the effectual working

that in the way of foreshadowing it was made known to the prophets, only not in such clearness as now. Paul indeed knew, and used on other occasions, the Old Testament anticipations of the universal grace of God; but here he is not thinking of these, but of the broad general contrast of the ages, especially as it is also a contrast between human ignorance and divine revelation. He then proceeds to state the contents of this mystery now made known.

6. *to wit*, **that the Gentiles are fellow-heirs, and fellow-members of the body, and fellow-partakers of the promise in Jesus Christ through the gospel,**] To feel the force of this, we must read in the word Gentiles its original meaning, nations, so that "the nations" really includes all the tribes of mankind. The revelation is not that they may be, or even that they shall be, but that they really are, all that is here said of them. It is actually true of many from among many nations, and these are viewed by Paul as representatives of the whole, while he eagerly anticipates the full realisation. In using three words compounded with the preposition "with," one if not two of them apparently coined by Paul himself, he indicates their association on equal terms with others. But he does not say "with the Jews," or "with us"; and to suppose that he means merely that the Gentiles have the same privileges as Israel, is to mistake the height of his thought, and to make it very unworthy of the lofty language he has been using. For, as he has shown before (ch. ii. 15-22) that both Jews and Gentiles are united by Christ into one new and higher community, with the most blessed access to God; it is that which he has in view here, in the fellowship of which he speaks. Such a unity of all the nations is indeed a thing well deserving to be celebrated as a wonderful revelation of God. They are fellows in three things, which are not mere repetitions of the same idea, but distinct and well arranged. First, they are fellow-heirs, *i.e.* of God, which shows the title they have to all spiritual blessings from the good will of the Father; next, they are called "fellow-members of the body," *i.e.* of the body of Christ, the united community of His people; and lastly, they are fellow-partakers of the promise, *i.e.* probably, the promise of the Holy Spirit. This threefold fellowship they have in Christ, as Paul has already fully shown how all blessings are in Him, since only in union with Him can they be enjoyed; and they have them through the gospel, the message of God's salvation in Christ, which is glad tidings to all the nations of the earth. That message, heard and believed, is the only and all-sufficient means by which we are made partakers of all these precious privileges.

7. **whereof I was made a minister, according to the gift of that grace of God which was given me according to the working of his power.**] The relative "whereof" refers to the gospel, just mentioned as the means by which all the nations might partake of all the blessings before described; and Paul now comes to speak of himself as not only having had the great secret made known to him (ver. 3), but having been made a minister of the glad tidings in which it is proclaimed. The word "minister" means simply servant, but, in distinction from other words of the same general significance,

> 8 of his power. Unto me, who am less than the least of all
> saints, is this grace given, that I should preach among the
> 9 Gentiles the unsearchable riches of Christ; and to make all

it denotes a servant with special reference to the work he has to do. The words usually rendered servant express rather his relation to his master. The work here pointed to is the conveying of the good tidings; and Paul very emphatically says that he was made an agent in this work by a gift of God's favour, bestowed on him according to the working of His power. In these words he refers to the great change that had passed upon him, when from being a violent persecutor of Jesus and His gospel, he became a believer and preacher of the faith which he once destroyed. This change he ascribes here, as always, to the mercy and the power of God; and he would have his readers consider, when he appeals to them, not what he might deserve in his own personal character, but what God in His almighty grace had done for him and by him. Hence this statement of his call to the ministry of the gospel prompts him to an adoring outburst of wonder and gratitude.

8. **Unto me, who am less than the least of all saints, was this grace given, to preach unto the Gentiles the unsearchable riches of Christ;**] With a bold defiance of grammar, he forms a comparative on the top of a superlative, giving in one word what is well expressed in our translation, "less than the least." He does not exclude himself from the number of the saints, *i.e.* the people of God, those truly and spiritually consecrated to Him; but he calls himself by far the least of them all. Nor will any Christian think this an exaggerated or insincere expression. In 1 Cor. xv. 9 he had called himself the least of the apostles, not worthy to be called an apostle, because he persecuted the Church of Christ. But here he is not merely thinking of that great outward sin, or of his relation to the other apostles, but of his general consciousness of his own unworthiness and sin, in contrast with the wonderful mercy and favour he had received. Looking at all together, his never forgotten career of bigotry and cruelty, his sense that in his flesh dwelt no good thing (Rom. vii. 15), his painful struggles with indwelling sin, he knew more evil in and about himself than he did of any other, and he could never fail to regard his forgiveness and favour as a marvel of God's mercy and love. So in 1 Tim. i. 15 he speaks of himself as the chief of sinners; and every believer who judges himself at all as Paul did, will be able to understand and enter into the confession. There does not seem to be any ground for regarding the three parallel statements as indicating the apostle's growth in humility, from the time of his First Epistle to the Corinthians to this one, and thence to the First Epistle to Timothy; still less for supposing that either of the latter is an exaggeration by an imitator of the undoubtedly genuine statement in 1 Cor. xv. 9. All alike express substantially the same sentiment in various aspects, and that sentiment is based on the most essential principles of Paul's teaching.

The favour granted him by God's mercy was to preach, or, more exactly, to declare as glad tidings, to the Gentiles the unsearchable riches of the Christ. Thus he describes the theme and nature of his message. Riches is a favourite word with Paul, and denotes overflowing fulness of every kind of good and blessing. Such fulness he intimates belongs to the Saviour, whom he has to proclaim and offer to men; and this very announcement is glad tidings to those who are, as he had previously described them, apart from Christ,

men see what *is* the fellowship of the mystery, which from the beginning of the world hath been hid in God, who created 10 all things by Jesus Christ: to the intent that now, unto the

most destitute and unhappy. The riches of Christ he here characterises as unsearchable, or that cannot be fully traced or tracked out; and so it is shown to be amply sufficient for every want that any man may have or feel. The business of the missionary is not to attempt fully to explain that which is unsearchable, but to proclaim as glad tidings the fact that it is so, and to offer to all men the Saviour who has this unsearchable riches, assuring them that they will find in Him a supply for all their needs, however great and various and peculiar these may be.

9. **and to make all men see what is the dispensation of the mystery which from all ages hath been hid in God who created all things;]** This is a further description of the apostle's calling and work, showing that it has a wider scope than even the evangelisation of the heathen, and that is the enlightenment of all men in regard to the purposes and ways of God. The Revisers here have made two changes in the A. V., both of which were required to make it agree with the oldest and best copies. The one is that instead of "fellowship" they have put "dispensation," so that the subject of enlightenment is not how we partake of the secret of God now revealed, but how God has ordered and arranged it. And the other change is the omission of the words "by Jesus Christ" at the end of the verse, so that the reference of the last clause is simply to God's having created all things, not to the more special truth, which Paul elsewhere teaches, that he did so through Jesus Christ His Son. The Revisers have also indicated in the margin that some ancient authorities omit "all men" in the first clause, and read simply in general "to bring to light." This, however, makes no material difference; and there is more probability for the text as it stands. The mystery or secret, as before stated, is Christ, as a Saviour in whom all men, Gentiles as well as Jews, are fellow-heirs, and fellow-members of His body, and fellow-partakers of the promise (vers. 4, 6); and this, he says, was from all ages hid. That is a stronger word than he had formerly used when he said it was not made known; it suggests a positive concealment, as a part of God's dispensation. But it suggests also, that the mystery was in existence and was unknown only because it was purposely hid from view. The great transition from the Jewish to the Christian dispensation, from the covenant with Israel to the new covenant in Jesus Christ, did not imply a change in God's character and will, but only the revelation of what had been always there. When the father received back his prodigal son, he did not then first begin to love him, or to give him an equal place in his affection with his elder brother; only the love and mercy he had for him all along, but could not express, were now revealed. So the union of all men in Christ was hid in God, and was really in His heart, even when in former ages He seemed to make Himself known only to Israel. The clause, "who created all things," seems to be added to indicate the supreme authority of God in disposing the course of the world's history, and the progress of His kingdom, according to His own wise and holy will. It may suggest, also, that He who has created all has kind and gracious feelings towards all the souls He has made, though for ages He might seem to be the God of the Jews only. The next clause indicates a purpose that has a still wider reach than has been yet stated.

principalities and powers in heavenly *places*, might be known
11 by the church the manifold wisdom of God, according to the

10. to the intent that now unto the principalities and the powers in the heavenly *places* might be made known through the church the manifold wisdom of God,] There has been some question as to what precisely it is which is said to have been done with this intent; since grammatically the clause may be connected with more than one of the preceding statements, *e.g.* with "created" or with "hid." But it is most natural to construe it with the main statement of the sentence, which is that expressed in vers. 8 and 9*a*, "to me ... was this grace given, to declare glad tidings to the Gentiles ... and to enlighten all." The revelation in Christ of the secret of God's grace is the chief thought in Paul's mind; and, after declaring how that brings glad news to the Gentiles, and enlightenment to all men, he goes on to say that it was designed also to give to beings of higher nature and order a greater knowledge of God than they would otherwise have. The words rendered "principalities and powers" are the same as those translated "rule and authority" in ch. i. 21, and plainly refer back to that passage. They denote superhuman beings, over whom it has been said before, Christ has been exalted; and the clause, "in the heavenlies," means, as before, the ideal place of abode to which Christ has been raised, and His people raised together with Him (chs. i. 3, 20, ii. 6). These higher intelligences have their knowledge of God increased "through the church," *i.e.* not by receiving teaching from the Church, for of that no hint is given, but by what they see of the formation, and growth, and character, and blessedness, of the community of believers in Jesus gathered together out of all nations of mankind. The attribute of God that he here declares is to be made known to the heavenly hosts, is His wisdom. Not as if that were the only aspect of the divine character that is illustrated by the salvation of sinful men; for he had before said that God designed to show in the ages to come the exceeding riches of His grace (ch. ii. 7). But, while that is specially manifested in His mercy and love to the sinful, considered by themselves; in the view Paul is here taking of the gathering into one fellowship of men whose previous characters and histories have been so different as those of the Jews and Gentiles, it is the wisdom of God that is most conspicuous. In exactly the same way Paul is led, in his epistle to the Romans, after explaining God's various dealings with Israel and the heathen nations, and showing how He has shut up all unto disobedience, that He might have mercy on all, to the adoring exclamation, "O the depth of the riches both of the wisdom and knowledge of God!" etc. (Rom. xi. 32-36). The train of thought is the same here, only expressed more briefly and calmly, and not with such an outburst of feeling. On the other hand, however, he rises higher here, by representing the wisdom of God as shown even to angelic minds. According to the representations of Scripture, the aspect of the divine character of which these superhuman intelligences have no direct knowledge is His mercy, as shown in the forgiveness and redemption of sinful and guilty creatures. This might well seem to them to be inconsistent with the holiness and justice that are declared to be manifested in God's dealings with the angels that sinned; and the observation of the history of the human race would raise questions and problems, such as men in all ages have found to be insoluble. But when it is seen how, in the salvation of sinners through Jesus Christ, God's righteousness no less than His love is revealed, and how the permission of sin and

eternal purpose which he purposed in Christ Jesus our Lord :
12 in whom we have boldness and access with confidence by

ignorance during so many ages has been made the means of bringing an innumerable company of men to such a sense of guilt as to accept Christ's redemption; we can understand how wisdom is the attribute specially signalised. It is called manifold, or, literally, much variegated; as it were some rich and skilfully woven piece of tapestry or embroidery, in which threads of many different colours are cunningly interlaced, in many various ways, so that, although when seen in parts or in an incomplete state it seems unsightly and without order, yet when finished it is perceived as a whole to present an artistic and beautiful picture. Such is the design that God's infinite wisdom is working out in what seems the tangled web of human history, in order to the revelation of His character and will, not to man only, but to multitudes of higher beings and other worlds.

11. **according to the eternal purpose (*Gr.* purpose of the ages) which he purposed in Christ Jesus our Lord:**] This clause repeats what had been said before in the beginning of the epistle (ch. i. 4), and teaches that the wisdom of God, while it is much variegated and acts differently at different times and seasons, does not do so, like the wisdom of men, because it changes with changing circumstances, but is constantly carrying out one great plan, in which all times and circumstances were foreseen, a purpose of the ages, formed before they began to roll, and stedfastly held and followed through all their changing course. This clause rendered "which he purposed" is, literally, "which he made"; and may either refer to the formation of the purpose in eternity, as our translators and Revisers have rendered it, or to the working out of it in time. The latter reference is favoured by the full historical title given to the Saviour, "Jesus Christ our Lord"; and it also gives a more distinct meaning to the statement, that it was wrought in Him. For although the name Jesus Christ, which properly describes Him as incarnate, is sometimes used of His pre-existent state (see Phil. ii. 5, 6), and though Paul has said before that we were chosen in Christ before the foundation of the world, yet it does not convey a very distinct idea to say that a plan was made in Christ, and the very elaborate naming of Christ as incarnate seems to point rather to the historical accomplishment of the eternal purpose of God. In Him, as the man Christ Jesus, our Lord and Saviour, God wrought that which He had purposed before all the ages, not only for our salvation, but for the manifestation of the glory of His grace to the universe. The form in which, according to the best authorities, our Saviour's name is here expressed is an uncommon one, and may be literally rendered "the Christ, even Jesus our Lord"; and His relation to us is more fully expressed in the next verse.

12. **in whom we have boldness and access in confidence through our faith in him.**] Paul has now come back from his lofty expatiation on the transcendent purpose of God, as made known after long ages to higher intelligences; and once more speaks of the actual experience of Christians in this life. He describes the nearness and intimacy which we have with God, in a remarkable fulness of expression. And well he may, since it is in Christ, of whom such glorious things have been spoken, that we have them. We have, he says, our boldness, for the word is definite, as pointing to something that his readers would know well. Boldness literally means freedom of speech, liberty to utter all that is in our heart without fear or shame. This is the privilege of those who are truly reconciled to God, who know that He forgives all their sins, and

13 the faith of him. Wherefore I desire that ye faint not at my
14 tribulations for you, which is your glory. For this cause

who therefore can and do with guileless heart confess all the guilt of which they are conscious, and do not shrink from His knowing all their feelings and desires. To this is added, our access or admittance, *i.e.* not merely the right or privilege of drawing near to God, but the actual enjoyment of it, the being introduced into His presence, further described by a third term as being in confidence, not with any doubtful hope, but with well-grounded assurance of our acceptance. We can come to God, not as slaves nor as criminals, with some vague and uncertain hope of pardon, but as children to a father, because we have this precious blessing in Christ, God's own Son. Paul adds that we have this boldness and access with confidence through our faith in (literally of) Christ, *i.e.* faith of which Christ is the object, which is the means of our union to Christ, and in virtue of which we are in Him. Observe that, while the apostle speaks of boldness and confidence as blessings competent to Christians as such, which he may simply assume that they possess, he does not identify any of them with saving faith, but mentions that distinctly as the means through which they are attained. Faith has Christ for its object, and is not a reflective or self-conscious act, but simply the trust of a guilty, perishing sinner in the Saviour; it is the root from which these conscious states of boldness and confidence naturally grow, but they may not be developed all at once, or they may be checked by biting blasts of trouble or doubt, even where there is real faith. Observe, too, that our boldness and confidence are not in our own faith, but in Christ. They are to be fostered and increased, not by looking inward to ourselves, and poring over our faith and experience, but by looking outward to Christ, so as to learn more of what He is, and has done, and is willing to do for us, and by such prayer as that which Paul proceeds to offer for his readers, after briefly exhorting them not to lose heart.

13. **Wherefore I ask that ye (*or* I) faint not at my tribulations for you, which are (*or* is) your glory.**] The word here rendered "ask" may denote a petition either to God or man; our "pray" would preserve the ambiguity; and as neither the object of "ask" nor the subject of "faint" is expressed, it may grammatically be taken in either sense; and some think, as indicated in the margin of R. V., that it is a prayer to God, in which case it must be for himself, since his prayer for his readers is given in the following verses. But this requires that the object after "ask" be different from that supplied before faint, which is not natural; and, after such a description of the greatness of his mission, it is not likely that Paul would indicate a fear of fainting. It seems every way better, therefore, to understand the verse, as our translators and Revisers have preferred, as an exhortation to the believers to whom he wrote, not to lose heart or become cowardly in following Christ, because he, the apostle of the Gentiles, was in chains and affliction on account of his preaching the gospel to them. This might well appear to the Gentile Christians of Asia to be a crushing defeat of their cause. Paul was at that time the one outstanding champion of the equal rights of Gentiles and Jews in Christ. The original apostles had no doubt recognised them in theory, and given Paul the right hand of fellowship; but they had still confined their preaching to the Jews; while Peter, and even Barnabas, had been weak enough to belie their principles in the face of Jewish bigotry. Paul's last mission to Jerusalem had been in large measure unsuccessful; there had been no strenuous effort on the part of the Jerusalem Church to save him from the

> I bow my knees unto the Father of our Lord Jesus Christ,
> 15 of whom the whole family in heaven and earth is named,

fury of their fellow-countrymen; nay, it was through his compliance with a somewhat doubtful advice of James and the elders that he had fallen a victim to it, and was now a prisoner at Rome. It might well seem that the project of a universal or catholic Church was a lost and hopeless cause, when its one champion had been baffled by Jewish bigotry, and was confined by Roman chains. They might be tempted to think that, if there was to be a religion to embrace all men, it must be based, not on the Messianic hopes of Israel, but on some universal philosophy that would embody the truth of all religions. This doubtless was a practical consideration that gave plausibility and currency to the incipient Gnostic speculations against which Paul warns the Colossians in his contemporaneous epistle to them; and to guard them against this, he had dwelt in the preceding verses on the lofty and far-reaching scope of the gospel that had been entrusted to him. With the inferential conjunction "wherefore," he now points back to the whole contents and main scope of the paragraph (vers. 2–12). Since I am a minister of an eternal purpose of God, long kept secret, but now revealed, which is glad tidings to all mankind, which enhances the knowledge even of the principalities and powers in heaven, and which gives you such blessed fellowship and boldness with God; will ye lose heart and courage, or become cowardly and desert the cause, merely because I, who am the messenger of such glad tidings, have to endure afflictions on that account? What I suffer is on your behalf. I do not grudge it; and you might consider it an honour to you. That I should endure these bonds, rather than abandon the cause of you Gentiles, shows how much I value you; and instead of letting this dishearten you, it should rather elate and encourage you. It is the work and purpose of God that I am carrying on; and whatever I may suffer, there is no fear but that it will finally prevail.

The marginal reading, "which is your glory," points to their not fainting as the antecedent; but this construction is not necessary, nor is it at all so natural. It is not so likely that Paul would appeal to their self-esteem by saying that it would be to their credit not to faint, as that he would point out that his very afflictions, which tended to dishearten them, were an honour to them.

Yet this request shows that he feels it to be not quite a light or easy thing for them to be stedfast, and therefore he assures them that he earnestly prays on their behalf, for such spiritual strength and insight into God's purpose of love, as will enable them to be of good courage.

14, 15. **For this cause I bow my knees unto the Father, from whom every family (*Gr.* fatherhood) in heaven and in earth is named,**] Paul uses the expression "I bow my knees" to express the humility and earnestness with which he offered his intercession for them, like the leper appealing to Jesus for healing (Mark i. 40), or the father pleading for his demoniac child (Matt. xvii. 14). And it need not be thought that he only offered such prayer at the time of writing this epistle; for, as he had said before that he continually made mention of them in his prayers (ch. i. 16), these petitions also would be frequently offered when the special considerations of which he has been speaking were before his mind.

In the next words, which indicate the character in which he invokes God, the Revisers have made two changes in the A. V. (1) On the authority of the oldest testimonies, they have omitted the words "of our Lord Jesus Christ" after Father, and in this omission all competent judges agree. (2) They have changed "the whole family" into "every family," an alteration which is not so universally admitted to be correct. The question turns on the same grammatical rule as applies to the words in ch. ii. 21, "the whole building" or "every building"; and although, according to rule, the absence of the article requires the translation "every," there are possible exceptions in the N. T., and it is contended by some that the sense requires us to admit one here. As before indicated, I am disposed to agree with those who take that view of ch. ii. 21; but the case is somewhat different here, for in this place the absence of the article is certain, whereas there it is not quite so; and more especially here the rendering "every" gives a good and worthy sense, whereas there the Revisers had to modify it in their text into "each several building." If the clause "of our Lord Jesus Christ" were genuine, the translation "the whole family" would give the better sense; but since we must omit them, the strict grammatical rendering gives a thought which, though unusual, is highly appropriate. The word rendered "family" is etymologically derived from "father," and though it is not used in the sense of the abstract "fatherhood" (R. V. margin), the connection might be expressed in English by using the phrase "father's house," which is a frequent Hebrew equivalent. And the phrase "of whom is named" does not mean merely "to whom belongs," but "from whom every father's house derives its name."

God is therefore invoked here as the Father absolutely, the origin and archetype of all fatherhood, wherever and whatever it may be. It is not as if the name Father were given to God merely by analogy, or figure of speech, borrowed from human family relations. That may be the way in which men have often given Him this name, or have risen to conceive of His character. But in reality it is the other way. God's fatherhood is the original and eternal pattern, of which all other fatherhood is a copy, more or less perfect. It has been thought strange and impossible that Paul should speak of separate families in heaven, *i.e.* among the angels; since Jesus said they neither marry nor are given in marriage. But the name father was anciently used with great latitude, *e.g.* of a prophet by his disciples, or of a king by his subjects, and Paul seems to have conceived of the angels as in some regular order, as principalities and powers; while, after all, his purpose here is not to describe them, but to say that wherever there is, or may be, a father's house of any kind, it is an efflux or shadow of the eternal fatherhood of God. To address God in this character was natural, not only as emphasising His greatness, but also His willingness to grant great things to them that ask Him. Whatever love, and tenderness, and pity, and care are found in any father towards his children, have all come from God, and are in absolute perfection in Him. So Paul approaches God in the spirit in which Jesus has taught us to pray, and with the plea that He has given us. "If ye, being evil, know how to give good gifts to your children, how much more will your heavenly Father give good things to them that ask him?" (Matt. vii. 11).

Then follows (in vers. 17–19) the petition of this prayer, which is essentially for strength, as the former (ch. i. 17–19) was for enlightenment. Only as the strength they needed was not physical, but moral, the apostle indicates the mental and religious conditions by which it is to be attained, and so his prayer branches out into several distinct clauses, all, however, conspiring towards the one great end in view.

16 that he would grant you, according to the riches of his
glory, to be strengthened with might by his Spirit in the inner
17 man; that Christ may dwell in your hearts by faith; that ye,
18 being rooted and grounded in love, may be able to comprehend with all saints what *is* the breadth, and length, and
19 depth, and height; and to know the love of Christ, which
passeth knowledge, that ye might be filled with all the fulness

16, 17*a*. that he would grant you, according to the riches of his glory, that ye may be strengthened with power through his Spirit in the inward man; that Christ may dwell in your hearts through faith;] Before expressing any particular request, Paul adds to the general introductory clause, "that he would grant you," the words "according to the riches of his glory," at once to show in how large a measure he desired the blessings he is about to name, and how worthy it would be of God to grant them. God's glory is the manifestation of His adorable character, and one aspect of it is seen in what has just been said, that every father's house in the universe is named after Him. Thus He, the eternal Father, is known and celebrated; and in accordance with what He has gloriously revealed Himself to be, as the perfect Father, He may be expected to bless His children.

The first request is "that ye may be strengthened with power . . . in the inward man." Strength of mind and heart was what they needed that they might not faint; firmness of resolution, stedfastness of purpose, in the face of danger or temptation. Such inward strength is, according to the uniform teaching of Scripture, given by the Spirit of God, as was seen most conspicuously in the case of the original disciples of Jesus after the descent of the Spirit on them on the day of Pentecost; and, accordingly, Paul prays that the Asian converts may be thus strengthened by God's Spirit. But since the Holy Spirit is the Spirit of Christ, and by the Spirit Christ Himself comes to His people, he joins with this petition another running parallel to it, "that Christ may dwell in your hearts through faith." The Spirit works by testifying of Christ, and so making Him really present to us through our faith. By that exercise of soul we see Him who is invisible, and realise a Saviour near us, yea in us, with whom we can have real and loving converse. Such was the way in which the disciples were strengthened and made courageous. The cause of their boldness was the inward working of the Holy Spirit; but that which consciously gave them ground of confidence was the assurance that their Lord and Saviour was living, and was with them, able and ready to help and support them. So Paul prays for his readers that Christ may dwell in their hearts, *i.e.* abide and have a home there, not merely be occasionally present. Wherever there is faith in Christ, He is present to the soul, and there is a bond of union formed that is permanent. But when faith is only exercised at intervals, this is obscured in our consciousness, and we only feel His presence at times; and when we forget, or do not look to Him, we are weak. What we need for strength is, that faith be in continual exercise, then Christ's conscious presence will be habitual, and we shall be strong and stedfast. But the apostle's prayer goes much further.

17*b*. to the end that ye, being rooted and grounded in love, (18) may be strong to apprehend with all the saints what is the breadth and length and height and depth, (19) and to know the love of Christ which passeth knowledge, that ye may be filled unto all the fulness

of God.] It is a question whether the clause, "ye, being rooted and grounded in love," should be construed, as it is both in the A. V. and R. V., as grammatically following the words "to the end that," and so connected with what follows, or taken as a nominative absolute, and joined with the preceding. The difference in meaning is not very great, and the best interpreters are divided; but, on the whole, the considerations in favour of the latter view seem to preponderate. On that construction the words express the condition and means of our being strengthened and Christ dwelling in our hearts. That is love, not the love of God or Christ to us, but love as exercised by us, love in general, as a disposition or principle, whether to God and Christ, or to our fellow-men. But the mere existence of love is not all: we are to be stedfast in it, like a tree deeply and firmly rooted in the earth, or a building firmly set on a solid foundation. That is to say, our love is not to be fitful and uncertain, varying with changing feelings or experiences, but firm and constant, because based on principle. It is not meant that our love is the root or foundation, but it is the sentiment in which we are to be steady and ever growing. The faith through which Christ dwells in our hearts works by love.

This firmness and growth in love is prayed for as the means of a further blessing, comprehensive knowledge of the things of God, "that ye may be strong to apprehend." The word is more exactly rendered by the Revisers "be strong," than "be able" in A. V.; for it is not the common word indicating merely possibility, but an unusual one which suggests that some vigour is needed to attain the object. Not, however, mere intellectual vigour, but the power that is given by love; for the essential nature of God, which is love, is apprehended only by those who have love in their own hearts (comp. 1 John iv. 7, 8). This knowledge is to be attained "with all the saints"; it is no private and peculiar experience of specially favoured individuals, whether distinguished by superior knowledge or ecstatic visions, which Paul desires they may have, but one in which all God's people, all those who are truly living for Him, whatever their rank or occupation in the world, may share. Only he would have them be inferior to no others, but be equal with them all in this blessed attainment. The object of the apprehension and knowledge is declared in two clauses, the former of which seems imperfectly expressed, as there is only a series of qualities, "what is the breadth, and length, and height, and depth," without an express mention of the thing to which these attributes belong. Some think that Paul has in his mind a different object from that which he names in the following clause; and one view is that it is the Christian Church, conceived as a great building, a holy temple to the Lord, as it has been described in ch. ii. 20–22. To those who think that the words with which Paul introduces this prayer, "for this cause" (ver. 14), refer back directly to that passage, it seems not unnatural to understand that idea here. But if any special object is to be supplied, the mystery or plan of God, more recently spoken of (ch. iii. 9–11), would be less far-fetched. Perhaps, however, it is more probable that the same object is meant here as in the following clause, "the love of Christ"; and that the apostle first mentions its infinite extent in all directions, in breadth as reaching over the whole world, in length as continuing from eternity to eternity, in depth as reaching down to the lowest degree of our sin and misery, in height as raising us up to the very throne of God; and then, feeling that it is not merely an apprehension of its greatness, in all these respects, but a direct knowledge of this love itself, that we need, adds the bold

20 of God. Now unto him that is able to do exceeding
abundantly above all that we ask or think, according to the
21 power that worketh in us, unto him *be* glory in the church
by Christ Jesus throughout all ages, world without end.
Amen.

paradox, " and to know the love of Christ that passeth knowledge," *i.e.* not
merely to know that it passeth knowledge, but to have real knowledge, in
experience, of that which, in its full extent, no creature can know.

The last and highest of the apostle's petitions in this wonderful prayer is
"that ye may be filled unto all the fulness of God." The fulness of God
undoubtedly means that of which He is full, the whole sum of excellences and
perfections that belong to the Divine Being, and make Him worthy of adoration, trust, and love. And here it is manifest, from the context, that the
moral attributes, in which we can resemble God, are meant, such as wisdom,
holiness, justice, goodness, love, and truth. Compare John i. 14-17, where
the fulness of Christ is summed up in grace and truth, and we are said to
receive out of His fulness grace for grace. The end of our knowing the love
of Christ, as Paul prays we may, is that we may be filled with such love in
our own hearts, beholding the glory of the Lord, we are changed into the
same image (2 Cor. iii. 18). This is our being filled, or made complete, such
likeness to God is what we were made for; as long as we have it not, we are
empty and incomplete, falling short of our ideal and plan. When we are
made strong by the Spirit, so that Christ abides in us, and we are rooted in
love, so as to know the love of Christ, our emptiness is gradually filled up, by
the growth and increase of those graces that are the fruits of the Spirit—love,
joy, peace, longsuffering, gentleness, kindness, faithfulness, meekness, temperance (Gal. v. 22, 23). And this process of filling Paul prays may go on,
until it reaches all the fulness of God, *i.e.* until all His communicable attributes have been bestowed on His children, in all the perfection which they
can receive, so that that word of Jesus may be fulfilled, which is at once a
precept and a promise, " Ye shall be perfect, even as your heavenly Father
is perfect " (Matt. v. 48).

The prayer contained in the previous verses is so bold, asking for such
great and unspeakable blessings, that the apostle adds to it a doxology, in
which he draws, from the infinite power and glory of God, the assurance
that we shall be heard even in such transcendent requests.

20, 21. Now unto him that is able to do exceeding abundantly above
all that we ask or think, according to the power that worketh in us,
unto him *be* the glory in the church and in Christ Jesus unto all
generations for ever and ever. (*Gr.* all the generations of the age of the
ages.) Amen.] Even so lofty a prayer is not beyond the power of God to
grant, for He is able to do far more than that. The phrase "exceeding
abundantly above all" well renders the exulting language of Paul, who, as is
his wont, heaps one comparative upon another in defiance of strict grammar.
" Above all " might satisfy an ordinary writer, but he adds " abundantly ";
and not content with that, he frames the redundant expression "over abundantly above all," so intense is his feeling of the gracious power of God.
Not only above our asking, but even above our thinking, is He able to do;
what a wonderful thought, following such a prayer! This gives us confidence,
not only that our requests can be granted, but that they shall be. For this

CHAP. IV. 1. I therefore, the prisoner of the Lord,) beseech you, that ye walk worthy of the vocation wherewith ye are called, transcendent power is one of which we have personal experience; it is "the power that worketh in us," *i.e.* the power that he had before prayed that they might know (ch. i. 19), and the working of which, in their quickening and conversion, he had described (ch. ii. 1-10). It is not, then, mere natural omnipotence, working by the forces which move and mould the material universe; but moral and spiritual influence, operating through mercy and love upon free and willing agents, by which God is able to bestow those inward blessings that have been asked, and even far more. And because that power is working in the hearts of Christians, the conviction that God is able assures us also that He will do above all that we ask or think.

All the more because the glory is His. In such doxologies we may take the verb, which is usually omitted, either as imperative or as indicative; and perhaps it is better to take it in the latter way here, "to him is the glory," the praise and honour of the whole work of our salvation. This is preferable, because in the next clause the glory is said to be alike in the Church and in Christ. We might pray that God may be honoured in the Church, but in Christ it is more fitting to declare that He is honoured. The A. V., "in the church by Christ," cannot be defended, because the preposition is exactly the same in both clauses, and the best authorities insert "and" to connect them and show that they are parallel. The Church had been mentioned just once before (ch. i. 22) as the body of which Christ is the head, and so glory is here ascribed to God, both in the body of His people, and in Him who is its Saviour and Head. The meaning is not simply that the Church and Christ give praise to God, for though that might be signified by "in the church," it could hardly be by "in Christ Jesus." Rather it is, that both the Church and its Head are themselves to the glory of God, because in them are revealed most fully His adorable perfections, He is glorified in them.

It is suitable to the intensity of the apostle's feeling that so lofty a doxology should close with a very emphatic expression of eternity. An age is a long and indefinite period of time, and sometimes the simple phrase, "unto the age," is used to denote everlasting duration. But here we have ages, and indeed so many of them, that as years make up ages so these successive ages themselves make "ages of ages"; and in all the parts of these inconceivable cycles, which may be measured by the generations of created beings, God's glory is to be seen in the Church and in Christ Jesus. The various biblical forms of expressing eternity do not convey substantially different meanings; but they often seem to be chosen in accordance with the tone of feeling in the writer's mind, as he sometimes desires merely to express it, and sometimes to call up to mind some particular feature of it, whether its final and conclusive character, which is best suggested by a brief abrupt form, or its immense extension, which the longer forms seek to depict. Here Paul would have us think, as he is thinking, of the great enhancement of the glory of God from its being continually seen as age after age rolls on without cessation or end.

With the Fourth Chapter begins a series of exhortations to Christian duty, founded on the great facts of redemption and Christian experience.

IV. 1-16. *Exhortation to loving unity.*

1. I therefore, the prisoner in the Lord, beseech you to walk worthily of the calling wherewith ye were called,] The appeal is introduced by

2 with all lowliness and meekness, with longsuffering, forbear-

"therefore," as an inference, not from the immediately preceding prayer and doxology, but from the former part of the epistle as a whole; and it is enforced and commended to their feelings by a renewed reference to his bonds, of which he had spoken more fully in ch. iii. 1, 13. "The prisoner in the Lord" is slightly different from "the prisoner of Christ Jesus" (ch. iii. 1), since "of" brings out especially the thought that Christ is the cause of his imprisonment; "in" expresses that it is as one who is in living union to the Saviour that he endures it. The word rendered "beseech" has hardly the notion of personal entreaty so much as that has; it is frequent in the N. T., and translated in most places "exhort"; and it includes the idea of an authoritative charge, as well as of an earnest desire. This appeal covers all the precepts that follow; and its immediate object is a general and comprehensive one, which indicates the principle that ought to rule all Christian conduct. That conduct, here described by a common biblical figure as a walk, is to be worthy of the believer's calling. The change in the R. V. from "are" to "were called" brings out that the reference is to that initial act of God by which they had been turned from darkness to light, and of which he had before prayed that they might know the hope, and the great power by which it had been effected (ch. i. 18, 19). He would have the whole course of the Christian life to be of a piece with its beginning (comp. Col. ii. 6, 7). This is a general rule, by which we may try our conduct and any intended action: Is it worthy of one who has been called by God to the fellowship of His Son Jesus Christ our Lord? But the apostle does not merely give this general principle; he goes on to apply and illustrate it in rich and beautiful details.

2. **with all lowliness and meekness, with longsuffering, forbearing one another in love;**] The quality of lowliness is indeed frequently commended by the Hebrew prophets and psalmists; but by the Greek moralists it was hardly regarded as a virtue at all. They perceived that for a man to behave, as if he were lower than he really is, or thinks himself to be, is unworthy meanness of spirit; and though they acknowledged it to be right that one who is really worthy of little should think himself so, they deemed it a higher virtue to be, and to consider oneself, worthy of great things. But a true knowledge of God, and of the real standard of moral goodness, shows that, judged by it, no man is worthy of praise in His sight; and therefore it is right and fitting that, being frail and sinful creatures, we should recognise ourselves to be such, and feel and act accordingly. Now this is true humility; and since the call of the gospel comes to us as dead by our sins, and we are saved entirely by God's free grace, if we would walk worthily of our calling, it must be with lowliness. Our humility before God will keep us from pride in relation to our fellow-men. "Meekness" is another specially Christian virtue. It is opposed to the temper that gets easily angry, and indulges in personal wrath. Now Christ has shown, by precept and example, the power and the blessing of a gentle and quiet disposition, not easily provoked, but willing to return good for evil; and the forgiveness that we need and receive from God in Christ teaches us to show like mercy to our brethren. "Longsuffering" is the continued and patient exercise of this meekness, when tried by repeated and persistent provocations; and it is exercised in "forbearing one another," not resenting or revenging injuries, but allowing them to pass, and restraining the outbursts of passion that they

3 ing one another in love; endeavouring to keep the unity of
4 the Spirit in the bond of peace. *There is* one body, and one
5 Spirit, even as ye are called in one hope of your calling ; one

provoke. Not without cause does Paul add to this last clause the qualification "in love." For there is a kind of forbearance that passes over offences with a smiling face, treasuring them up all the while with secret malice in the heart, and only biding its time for a more terrible revenge, like Absalom's on his brother Amnon. Such forbearance is the very opposite of Christian, and is worse than passionate wrath. The forbearance that is Christlike and Godlike must have its motive in love. We are to refrain from retaliation on those who may do us wrong, not merely from prudence or pride, but from Christian affection, because we really wish them well. "One another" may have special reference to the Christian brotherhood immediately to be described ; and in this aspect it shows that we must be prepared for provocations from them as well as from the ungodly; but it is not to be limited to Christians, but extends to all men.

3. **giving diligence to keep the unity of the Spirit in the bond of peace.**] The alteration in the R. V. of "endeavouring" into "giving diligence" brings out the meaning better, for it is not a mere aim at an object doubtful of attainment, but zealous active work for what may and ought to be secured, that Paul here inculcates. That object is the maintenance of the unity of the Spirit, *i.e.* the oneness among the disciples of Christ that is wrought by the Holy Spirit of God. This is presented as a thing that really exists, but that is in danger of being broken, if believers do not walk with the lowliness, meekness, and loving forbearance that become their calling. "The bond of peace" is taken by some to refer to love, as that which binds or secures peace ; but it is much more natural to understand it of peace itself, as the bond by which the unity of believers is preserved, or more precisely, in which it consists. They are one in so far as there is peace among them all.

There follows a series of brief emphatic statements in which are enumerated the many things that Christians have in common, so as to show that everything by which they are such gives reason for the call to preserve the unity wrought by the Spirit.

4. *There is* **one body, and one Spirit, even as also ye were called in one hope of your calling**;] The body is the Church, the community of believers in Christ, which Paul had before called His body (ch. i. 22); and here he emphasises the fact that it is one. Though the name Church was given to each of the various congregations in widely distant places, yet all these make up together, not a mere aggregate of distinct societies, but one whole, which is the body of Christ. The Spirit, which he had just mentioned as the author of unity, is also now declared to be one ; and the unity must extend not only to all the members of a local congregation, but to all believers in Jesus. Just as the natural body is a single whole, though composed of many parts, because it is all animated by one living soul; so Paul conceives the mystical body of Christ to be one, because the one Spirit of God dwells in all its members. And he adds a confirmation of this from believers' own experience: "even as also ye were called," *i.e.* when ye were brought to faith in Christ, "in one hope of your calling." This points back to what he had said before of the hope of their calling (ch. i. 18) as a thing they were to be enabled by the Spirit to know. That hope is the same for all believers,

6 Lord, one faith, one baptism, one God and Father of all, who
7 *is* above all, and through all, and in you all. But unto every
and its object is to be made fellow-citizens of the saints, and of the household of God. Since all are called to the same hope, it is plain that all are one body, animated by one Spirit.

5. **one Lord, one faith, one baptism,**] These are further marks and proofs of unity. All Christians own allegiance and yield obedience to one Master, even Jesus Christ, whom by the Spirit they are moved and enabled to call Lord. Still further, there is one faith. By this is not meant the object of faith, or the doctrine of the gospel, for it is very doubtful whether the word ever has that meaning in the N. T., and it would be out of place here. It is, as usually, the act or exercise of soul by which we receive and rest upon Christ as our Saviour. Though there is one Lord, yet if the relation of different persons or classes to Him were different, if some had to look to Him merely with admiration and love, as the holy angels may do, while others had to trust Him for salvation, the union would not be perfect. But now all alike must come to Christ as sinners needing pardon, and all alike accept Him as their Redeemer, and trust Him for their acceptance with God : there is one faith. And there is also one baptism : the outward rite, that is the sign and seal of our union to Christ by faith, is one and the same for all. If some believers were to be initiated by circumcision, and others by baptism, this would constitute a difference such as was between Jews and proselytes in Israel. But since one simple and significant rite is the sign to all of their cleansing through fellowship by faith with the one Lord, there is no occasion or pretext for division in the unity of the Spirit.

But the apostle traces the motives and grounds of Christian unity still higher.

6. **one God and Father of all, who is over all, and through all, and in all.**] The R. V. has followed the best authorities in omitting the pronoun "you" in the last clause, as an addition meant to bring out that the reference is to Christians. However, the context seems to show distinctly that it is of them that Paul is speaking, since in ver. 4 he speaks of "your calling," and in ver. 7 writes "each one of us." The word "all" is as indefinite in the original as in the English translation, and in the last three clauses might mean " all things." But in the first clause it must be persons of whom God is said to be Father, and that makes it clear that persons must also be meant in the others. Since the Gentile believers are of the household of God, He is Father of all Christians, to whatever nation they may belong; and thus they are united as having, not only one Lord Jesus Christ, but one Father, who is God, and who is most closely related to every one of them. That relation is described as threefold. He is over all as supreme Ruler, Creator, and Preserver. He is through all, inasmuch as He employs all as instruments of His activity, working out His purposes, and revealing His character and will by means of them. He is in all, since He abides by His gracious presence in the hearts of all His children. This the best expositors agree to be the immediate import of these words. But some think there may also be in them a reference to God's relation in Christ to all men as such, in virtue of His transcendent fatherly love over all, " the co-extensiveness of redemption by the Son with the whole nature of man" (Alford), and the inward striving of the Spirit with all. But it is hard to see how that meaning could be expressed by the words "through all." And in general it is best

one of us is given grace according to the measure of the
8 gift of Christ. Wherefore he saith, When he ascended up
on high, he led captivity captive, and gave gifts unto men.

not to suppose a double meaning or reference, when the direct and simple one is natural.

Many expositors, including some of the earliest fathers and some of the best modern scholars, think that in the three clauses of this verse there is a reference to the three persons in the Godhead, so that God is above all in the person of the Father, through all in the person of the Son, and in all in the person of the Holy Spirit. This interpretation accords with the language of Trinitarian orthodoxy; but it seems rather forced as an exposition of the words of Paul, who teaches, indeed, the substance of the truth afterwards expressed in the ecclesiastical formulæ, but does not employ their technical language. Here, too, he has distinctly mentioned the Spirit (ver. 4) as animating the body of believers, and the Lord (ver. 5) as ruling it, and in this verse he is speaking of the Father. All that He says is true of Him; He works through believers (1 Cor. iii. 5–9), and He dwells in them (Eph. ii. 22). So that it seems better to regard all that is said here as referring to the Father, with whom the Lord and the Spirit have been associated in the preceding verses.

After this emphatic description of the unity of the Church, Paul proceeds, as he does also in other epistles (Rom. xii. 4–8; 1 Cor. xii. 4–31), to show that this does not imply absolute uniformity or similarity of all the parts, but, on the contrary, as in the natural body, diversity of functions, all combining to the maintenance and growth of the one organism.

7. **But unto each one of us was the grace given according to the measure of the gift of Christ.**] The R. V. follows the best authorities in inserting the definite article before grace, and gives a more exact rendering of the verb by putting it in the past tense, "was given." The grace that is meant is the favour or blessing of being made members of the spiritual body of Christ, and this was given to each at a definite point of time, when they were quickened from their death in sin, and brought to faith in Jesus. All believers may not be able to say when that blessed time was in their case, but all recognise that they owe their being in a state of salvation to the free undeserved mercy of God. Of this grace two things are said in this verse. First, that it is given to each believer in definite measure, so that they are not all absolutely alike in gifts and functions, though all have the grace of being members of Christ; and second, that these differences are determined by Christ. Of these two statements, the second is established in vers. 8–10, and the first in vers. 11, 12. For it was natural that the apostle should first convince his readers that the differences among Christians are due, not to mere chance, nor to personal excellence, but to the appointment of the one Lord Jesus Christ, whom they all trust; and then should show what these differences are, and how they are the means of the fuller growth and more perfect unity of the Church. Accordingly, the next verses are designed to show that the dispenser of these gifts is Christ; and this is done by quoting and commenting on a passage from O. T. Scripture.

8. **Wherefore he saith,**
    When he ascended on high, he led captivity captive,
    And gave gifts unto men.]
The quotation is introduced in a way common in the N.T., by the indefinite

9 (Now that he ascended, what is it but that he also descended
10 first into the lower parts of the earth? He that descended

phrase "saith," no nominative being expressed. In all such cases we are to understand "the Scripture," or "the Holy Spirit," or "God," as the subject, these three forms of expression being equivalent in meaning, since the N. T. writers regarded the O. T. as breathed by God.

The quotation is from Ps. lxviii. 18, which in the original runs thus: "Thou hast ascended on high, thou hast led captivity captive; thou hast received gifts among men." The change of person from "thou" to "he" is obviously a purely formal one, not affecting the meaning in the least; but the alteration of "received gifts among men" to "gave gifts to men," is startling, and has given rise to much perplexity; and many different explanations have been given of it. Paul's rendering is also that of the Chaldee paraphrase, and therefore probably was that adopted by the Jewish Rabbis; so that Paul is not alone in giving the passage this turn. The literal translation of the LXX. is obscure, even when read in the connection of the Psalm, and would have been quite unintelligible in the quotation here. For this is one of many passages in that Psalm that present difficulties in their exact interpretation, though the general scope and meaning of the poem are plain enough. It is a song of battle and victory for the people of God against His and their enemies. At what time, or for what victory, it was composed is not certain, for the description is mostly figurative, and God's interposition for the deliverance of Israel is presented by allusions to the Exodus from Egypt and the conquest of Canaan. On the principle that all divine deliverances in former times are types and foreshadowings of the great salvation wrought by Jesus, Paul applies it to His work. The verse he quotes describes the triumph of Jehovah, who is represented as having come from heaven to earth for the rescue of His people, and now, having accomplished that, ascending in a victorious march. Similarly God's coming down is described in Ps. xviii. 9-17; and His returning on high in Ps. vii. 7, xlvii. 5. "Thou hast led captivity captive" means "led in triumph a great multitude of captives." Then the gifts mentioned in the next clause would be the spoils taken from the enemy, which, however, are conceived as distributed, according to custom, among those on whose behalf Jehovah is triumphant (see Ps. lxviii. 12). The passage is thus a boldly figurative description of God, as a human conqueror, leading His enemies in triumph, and enriching His people with their spoils; and Paul gives a translation, which would seem to have been then current, and which expresses better for his purpose than a literal one could have done, the substantial meaning of the original. The question has been raised, who are the captives whom Paul has in view in his typical application of the Psalm, and many fanciful answers have been given. But it is not certain that he had in his mind any definite analogue to this part of the quotation; for he does not explain or refer to it at all, and the type is not an allegory, in which each particular has a symbolic meaning. But if we do pursue the typical application to this point, the captives can only be our spiritual enemies, the principalities and powers, over which Christ is said in the sister epistle to have triumphed (Col. ii. 15).

9. (**Now this, he ascended, what is it but that he also descended into the lower parts of the earth?**] Paul here states something as being implied in the expression "he ascended," namely, a descending also. The A. V. inserts "first" after "descended"; and the R. V. gives it in the margin as the

is the same also that ascended up far above all heavens, that
reading of some ancient authorities; but the weight of evidence is against it.
However, it just expresses what almost all expositors recognise as the meaning,
that the assertion of an ascent of God implies a previous descent. The apostle's
aim in remarking this may be conceived as twofold. He may have meant to
show that the quotation from the Psalm really referred typically to Christ.
The force of his inference depends on the fact that the words are spoken to
God, and that when He is said to have ascended He must be conceived as
having first come down to save His people. Now, such a descent, which was
ideally ascribed to God by the psalmists, has really been accomplished in the
self-emptying and humiliation of Christ (cf. 2 Cor. viii. 9; Phil. ii. 6–8). To
Him, therefore, all that is said of ascending and bestowing gifts most truly
and perfectly applies. This is a legitimate and appropriate application; and
some think that Paul's purpose does not go beyond this. But he is not in the
habit of justifying so elaborately his use of O. T. types in reference to Christ,
and the emphasis with which he repeats the idea in the next verse seems to
show that he designed also to bring out the gracious nature of Christ's distribution of the gifts of grace to His people, by pointing out the condescension
and humiliation through which He attained the right to bestow them.

This has an important bearing on the decision between two interpretations
of the last clause, each of which is supported by some of the best scholars,
though all admit that both are grammatically possible. "The lower parts of
the earth" is the equivalent of a Hebrew phrase, which in Ps. lxiii. 9 denotes
the under world, the abode of the dead, more commonly called Sheol in O. T.
and Hades in N. T. (improperly rendered "hell" in A. V.). But it may
also mean simply the earth, as a lower region compared with heaven; and
there are passages in O. T. where it is so used (Isa. xliv. 23 and Ps. cxxxix.
15 figuratively). Paul uses the phrase nowhere else; and the question is,
whether he means by it Christ's descent to earth at His incarnation, or His
going to the place or state of departed spirits at His death. Now, if Paul's
purpose be simply to justify his application of the Psalm to our Lord, the
former would seem the more natural explanation, for the descent of Jehovah,
that is implied in it, can only be to the earth, where He accomplished the
deliverance of His people, and it would be unwarrantable to infer from it
Christ's descent to the under world. This is the strongest argument for the
reference being simply to the coming of our Lord on earth. But if the apostle
did not so much feel it necessary to establish by a logical argument his right
to use the quotation, as desire to bring out the greatness of the grace in which
Christ bestows His gifts, it was quite proper that he should go beyond the
precise inference from the Psalm, in describing the depth to which He actually
descended. Then, since he speaks elsewhere of Christ being raised up from
the abyss, meaning the state of the dead (Rom. x. 7), and since the contrast in the
next verse is not merely with heaven, but with "far above all heavens," the
weight of probability seems to be on the side of this interpretation. Thus
Paul would remind his readers that our Lord not only humbled Himself for
our salvation, to be born, and to live as a man on the earth, but even to die,
and to continue in the state of the dead and under the power of death for a
time. This is what is meant by the clause in the Creed, "he descended into
Hades," and this along with other passages in N. T. show the truth of it.

10. He that descended is the same also that ascended far above all
the heavens, that he might fill all things.)] The words "the same" are

11 he might fill all things.) And he gave some, apostles; and some, prophets; and some, evangelists; and some, pastors
not a perfectly exact rendering of the original, which literally runs thus, " he that descended himself also is he that ascended," expressing still more emphatically the unity of the person. And the fact that the descent is now put first, confirms the view that the apostle is not thinking mainly of the inference from the Psalm, but of the great reality of which it presents a type. He would bring out that the Lord, who bestows on each of us a definite gift of His grace, is the Saviour who "humbled himself and became obedient unto death, even the death of the cross." The height of His exaltation is indicated by one of Paul's double comparatives, "far above," literally over above, "all the heavens"; and the meaning is the same as in ch. i. 21, 22, that Christ is raised to supreme glory and dominion, above every created being. There were then, and have been since, imaginative speculations about successive celestial regions, each rising above the former in blessedness; but the apostle does not intend to teach anything positive about these, but simply to declare that whatever they are, our Lord has ascended far above them all. Then he adds the ultimate purpose of this, which is, " that he might fill all things," the same idea as is expressed in ch. i. 23 (where see note). Here, as there, "all things" must be understood in the most extensive sense, so as to include the whole universe; and "fill" must mean to occupy with His presence. From this passage an argument has been drawn for the doctrine of the omnipresence of Christ's glorified human nature. For since the Deity is always omnipresent, it can only be the humanity of our Saviour that becomes so by His exaltation. It may be doubted, however, whether such an abstract metaphysical conception is akin to the thought of Paul here. He is emphasising the oneness of the descending and ascending Lord. By His descent He has become our Saviour, and by His ascending far above all the heavens He is everywhere present in that character, and fills all the universe, in the grace and love and saving power that are manifested in His incarnation and life on earth, and death on the cross. This is the ubiquity that is of value to us in our religious life, to be assured that everywhere and at all times the loving heart of Jesus, as He lived among men, is with us, not merely to accept a mysterious doctrine about the presence of His body.

In the English Bible, both A. V. and R. V., vers. 9 and 10 are marked as a parenthesis, so that ver. 11 is connected directly with the quotation in ver. 8. But this is a needless interruption of the train of thought; and the emphatic position of "he," literally "himself," at the beginning of ver. 11, indicates rather a reference to ver. 10. It is the very person who has descended so low to obtain our salvation, and then ascended so high to bestow it, who distributes the gifts that have been alluded to in ver. 7, and are now to be mentioned more in detail.

11. And he gave some *to be* apostles; and some, prophets; and some, evangelists; and some, pastors and teachers;] The consideration of who it is that has given the various gifts which the members of the Church of Christ enjoy, shows the sovereign authority, the infinite wisdom, and the abounding grace with which they are dispensed, and may well make each of us content and happy with the function He assigns us. Instead of mentioning, as gifts, the spiritual qualifications or endowments bestowed on men, He mentions the men themselves, who fill various offices, as the gifts of Christ. And the R. V. has made it plain to the English reader, as it is in the original,

that the meaning is, not, "to some he gave apostles," etc., but "he gave some men to be apostles," etc. To whom are they given? To men (ver. 8), to the whole Church in the first place, and ultimately to all mankind; yea, to the rebellious also. This verse asserts the great Christian principle, that the officials in the Church are not lords, but servants; the Church does not exist for them, but they for the Church, yea, for the world; for, like Paul, they are debtors both to Jews and Greeks, both to wise and unwise (Rom. i. 14). Their commission from Him who filleth all things, and has all authority in heaven and on earth, extends to all the nations (Matt. xxviii. 18, 19).

The enumeration of Christ's gifts here is parallel to two others in earlier epistles of Paul (Rom. xii. 6-8; 1 Cor. xii. 28-30). They all occur in connection with the idea of the diversity of the members in the one body of Christ; and there is a general similarity in them all, along with certain characteristic differences. In Rom. xii. it is diligence in the use of the talents assigned to each that is inculcated, and accordingly the reference is not to offices, but to various powers and means of doing good. In 1 Cor. xii. there is a special warning against arrogance and jealousy among those gifted in different degrees, and so the qualifications for the various offices are mentioned. Here the unity and harmony of the Church is the main theme; and the men, who in various functions serve the same great end, are described as gifts of the one Lord. In Rom. xii. apostles are not mentioned, since their duties are practically covered by the others mentioned; but in 1 Cor. xii., and here, they are named first, as the primary Christian workers. They are those who most directly received their commission from Christ, who were eye-witnesses of His resurrection, and were His ministers for the whole Church. Next in both these lists, and first in Rom. xii., come prophets, *i.e.* men so endowed with the Spirit of God that they spoke with divine insight and authority, whether about the past, the present, or the future. Then we have here a name absent from both the other lists, evangelists. This title is given by Paul to Timothy (2 Tim. iv. 5), and in Acts xxi. 8 it is applied to Philip, who, though at first appointed as one of the seven who had charge of the distribution of alms in the Jerusalem Church, after the dispersion on the death of Stephen acted as a herald of the gospel in Samaria and elsewhere. Most probably, therefore, the name denotes what we now call a missionary, one who, without being an apostle or a prophet, gave his life to the work of proclaiming the glad tidings where it was not yet known, and of preaching and organising new churches. This work fell to the apostles in the earliest days; but, as they passed away, it is natural that the evangelists, who continued it after them, should be more mentioned in the later N. T. writings. Then come "pastors and teachers," here classed together as one set of men, with the twofold function of ruling, expressed by the figure of shepherds leading the flock, and of teaching. In Rom. xii. those who teach and those who rule are both mentioned, and in 1 Cor. xii. "teachers" and "governments." The two functions were not always conjoined in the same persons, but they frequently were; and in 1 Tim. v. 17 we read of the elders (presbyters) who rule and also labour in the word and in teaching. The reference, therefore, seems to be to the presbyters, also called bishops (overseers); whom we learn to have been in all the congregations of the early Church. The enumeration is not pursued further here, for in none of the places is it meant to be formal or exhaustive; and the other endowments mentioned in the earlier epistles, miracles, healing, tongues, in 1 Cor., and giving, ministering, showing mercy, in Romans, were not possessed by special classes of men, and so were less appropriate to Paul's purpose here,

12 and teachers; for the perfecting of the saints, for the work
of the ministry, for the edifying of the body of Christ:
13 till we all come in the unity of the faith, and of the knowledge of the Son of God, unto a perfect man, unto the
14 measure of the stature of the fulness of Christ: that we

though suitable to his slightly different aims in the other places. He has shown sufficiently that all the men who are enabled to do any service to their fellows in Christian life are to be regarded as gifts of the once crucified but now exalted Saviour; and he now proceeds to point out what is the great purpose for which they are all given.

12. **for the perfecting of the saints, unto the work of ministering, unto the building up of the body of Christ:**] The R. V. shows the difference of the prepositions by which these clauses are introduced; and this makes it impossible to take them as all co-ordinate, describing three parallel aims. But there are two possible ways of connecting them. Some think that "for," which begins the first clause, indicates the remoter end, and that the two following clauses express the more immediate means by which it is to be attained. This is a distinction that the prepositions sometimes have; and so the meaning would be, that the work of ministering and the building up of the body of Christ are means for the perfecting of the saints. This would make the completion of the whole a means to the perfection of the individuals, which is hardly in keeping with the main line of thought here, though it is not opposed to Paul's general teaching. But it is noticeable that the word "perfecting" here is an uncommon one, and properly means fitting or adapting; so that another possible way of connecting the clauses is, to make the latter two depend on the first, "for the perfecting of the saints unto work of ministering," *i.e.* that they may be fitted or prepared for it. It is objected, that this would make the ministering a function of all the saints, and so a very indefinite thing. But the words are very indefinite, since there is no article corresponding to "the" in the English; it is simply "work of ministering"; and it is a thoroughly Pauline thought that all Christians are to be trained and fitted for the Christlike work of serving others. Why else does Paul change his figure here, and instead of saying, "unto the building up" of the temple of God, substitute "of the body of Christ"? Does not that show that he has in view their further employment? A body is nourished and built up in order that it may be active in worthy functions; and the Church, as Christ's body, even when perfected, cannot be conceived as an end in itself, but is to be employed in ministering to the good and salvation of others. Where and how this is to be done, neither Paul nor any other inspired teacher has told us, and conjectures are vain; but the truth of the idea in general is indicated by all the principles of the kingdom of God, as taught by Christ and His apostles. And the following verses (13–16) show that Paul has here before him very definitely the idea of the body of Christ, not only as a unity, but as a well-compacted organism, fit for healthful and vigorous activity.

13. **till we all attain unto the unity of the faith, and of the knowledge of the Son of God, unto a full-grown man, unto the measure of the stature of the fulness of Christ:**] This verse indicates the point up to which the various offices in the Church are to be continued. As they are means to an end, they are not everlasting; but exist only until their end is attained; and

henceforth be no more children, tossed to and fro, and carried about with every wind of doctrine, by the sleight of men, *and* cunning craftiness, whereby they lie in wait to deceive;

that end, before indicated, is here more fully described. When all the members of Christ are made fully perfect, the special work of the several ministers, through whom they believed and grew in grace, shall be superseded; for all shall be fitted to minister to one another, and to those who may be outside.

The change in the R. V. from "in" to "unto the unity of the faith, and of the knowledge of the Son of God," is a necessary correction; for the view, once held even by good scholars, that the preposition might have that meaning, is now exploded. Resort was had to that idea, no doubt, because Paul had already said "there is one faith" (ver. 5), and it seemed strange that he should now represent unity of faith as a thing still to be aimed at in the future. But while the faith of all Christians is the same in its nature and in its object, trust in the one Lord Jesus Christ, the apostle fully recognises its differences in degree and in enlightenment in different believers. Some are weak in faith and some strong, and this is a frequent cause of disputes and divisions (Rom. xiv. 1–xv. 7). These differences are to be borne with now; but ultimately, with the progress of the Christian life, they shall be done away. The mention of faith here, as that in which unity is to be attained, shows how truly that is the root of all Christian graces, so that real growth must ever be a growth in faith. With that is associated knowledge, full acquaintance, as the word literally means, not mere superficial apprehension. And the object of both is the Saviour, described here by his loftiest and most divine title, "the Son of God." The attainment of such faith and knowledge is then depicted in a parallel clause as a coming to maturity. The body of Christ is conceived as having a gradual growth, like the natural body, and coming at last to full and perfect stature. And the measure of its perfection is that it is to be the fulness of Christ, a complement worthy and fit for such a head. This is the glorious consummation, which shall render needless the services of any particular believers as pastors and teachers of their fellows, when they shall no more teach every man his neighbour, saying, Know the Lord; for they shall all know Him, from the least to the greatest. Till then, the distinction of offices and functions is to continue; and Paul goes on to say that it is to continue for the very purpose of bringing about that great end.

14. **that we may be no longer children, tossed to and fro and carried about with every wind of doctrine, by the sleight of men, in craftiness, after the wiles of error;**] There has been some discussion as to what particular clause in the context this statement of purpose refers to; but the most natural construction is to refer it to the main statement of the paragraph (in vers. 11, 12), that Christ has given as gifts to men, apostles, prophets, evangelists, pastors, and teachers. The negative side of the purpose is here expressed, that we be no longer children, literally "infants." The apostle has explained in 1 Cor. xiv. 20, that there is a sense in which he desires Christians to be always children, in respect of malice; he would always have them to be docile, confiding, loving; but here, as there, he indicates that in understanding they should be men. And he points out the danger of their not being so. They would be liable to vacillation and changes, according as they might be swayed in one direction or another by external influences, and

15 but, speaking the truth in love, may grow up into him in all
16 things, which is the head, *even* Christ: from whom the whole

so would make no steady progress. He illustrates this by the same figure as James uses for an imperfect faith (Jas. i. 6), of being tossed by waves, and driven hither and thither by every chance gust of wind. These winds consist of doctrine, *i.e.* teaching, what anyone professing to be wise and knowing may offer as instruction. In those days there was an immense number and variety of such persons, with all sorts of different views of life; and so it is also in our day. But besides the danger of teaching that is simply mistaken, there is also that of sophistry. The word rendered "sleight" is literally "dicing," and from that it has come to mean sleight of hand in so using the dice as to cheat with them; and "craftiness" is literally a readiness to do everything, unscrupulousness that will stick at nothing, but pursue its aim by all means fair or foul. This has too often been the sin of reckless controversialists and partisans. The clause, "after the wiles of error," means going after or tending to what is so designated by a very uncommon word used in N. T. only here and in ch. vi. 11, "the wiles of the devil." It denotes a plan or stratagem; and error is almost personified, as a great and dangerous opponent, into whose snare the mistakes and sophistries of men tend to drive immature believers. But the whole context plainly shows that it is not mere intellectual or speculative error of which Paul is so greatly afraid, but such as leads to licentiousness of life. And the next verse shows the positive safeguard to be of a moral nature.

15. **but speaking truth (*or* dealing truly) in love, may grow up in all things into him, which is the head, *even* Christ;**] "Speaking truth" is one word, and contains no special expression for speech, so that "dealing truly" is better, and perhaps Wyclif's "doing truth," though uncouth, is most exact of all. It would seem to denote what Jesus designates as "being of the truth," "doing truth" (John iii. 20, xviii. 37), *i.e.* having a sincere and earnest desire to know and follow the truth, whatever it may be, though humbling and distasteful. For, as Whately says, "everyone desires to have truth on his side, but it is not everyone who sincerely and earnestly desires to be on the side of truth." But this disposition is the only real security against error and deception, and the only guarantee of genuine progress.

The words "in love" are thought by some of the best expositors to be connected with the following verb, "may grow up," as they are similarly used in the end of the next verse. But it seems more natural here to construe them with the preceding participle. For there may be a truthfulness that is not loving, but stern, cynical, unsocial, which would not contribute to Christian growth. Hence Paul may well indicate that our doing truth must be tinged and saturated with love, not specially either to God, or Christ, or our fellows, but the temper of love in general, going out in all directions. Such truthful dealing will promote growth in all respects, more particularly in the faith and knowledge before mentioned, into Christ, *i.e.* into ever closer and more vital union with Him, as we become more and more of one mind and heart. He is here expressly viewed as the head: and the next verse reminds us that as the healthy growth of the material body does not consist merely in its increase in size, but in the harmony and normal working of all its parts; so the spiritual progress of the Church, as the body of Christ, depends on the living union of all its members with Him the head. The thought and phraseology here are the same as in the parallel Epistle to the Colossians, ii. 19; and since in that

body fitly joined together and compacted by that which every joint supplieth, according to the effectual working in the measure of every part, maketh increase of the body, unto the 17 edifying of itself in love. This I say therefore, and testify in the Lord, that ye henceforth walk not as other Gentiles walk,

place this vital connection with the head is set forth as the safeguard against the special errors that threatened the faith of that Church, there may be, as some think, a reference to them underlying the general mention of the system of error spoken of in ver. 14. Paul undoubtedly, at the time he wrote this epistle, had a knowledge of that particular form of so-called philosophy that had appeared at Colossæ, though in writing to Churches that may have been as yet ignorant of it he does not directly attack it, but gives general precepts which serve to guard against any form of anti-Christian speculation.

16. from whom all the body fitly framed and knit together through that which every joint supplieth (*Gr.* through every joint of the supply), according to the working in *due* measure of each several part, maketh the increase of the body unto the building up of itself in love.] This verse appropriately closes the paragraph (vers. 1–16) by summing up all that it contains of exhortation to Christian unity in a description of the growth and vigour of a healthful body. Its parts are many and various; but these are all articulated one to another, and united to the head, the special organ of the living soul that animates and moves them all: each has something to contribute to the welfare of the others, each acts in measure and proportion, and thus there is an organic growth, not merely by aggregation from without, but by inward assimilation and incorporation. This, which is a striking description of the marvellous structure of our bodily frames, giving evidence by numberless intricate adaptations of infinitely wise design, is metaphorically an image of the Church of Christ in its ideal state, each member in living union with Him, each having some function to discharge and some benefit to convey, none jarring or opposing another, but all together serving and increasing the whole.

IV. 17–V. 21. *Exhortation to Christian living.*—Paul now resumes the exhortation begun in vers. 1–3 after what might seem a digression, though it is really an expansion of the thought, and, so far from leading him away from his main line of address, helps him onward to the next stage of it. He had urged his readers to walk worthily of their calling as Christians, especially in lowliness, meekness, and loving unity; and had shown how these graces specially became them, as members of the living, organic body of Christ, which thrives and grows through the harmonious working of every part. The thought of this Christian community, however, reminds him that it exists in the midst of society of a very different character, and that they need to be warned against the habits and modes of life of that society. Accordingly, his precepts now take an antithetic form, and inculcate Christian virtues in opposition to heathen vices. Even genuine believers in Jesus could not all at once shake themselves free from previous habits and customary practices; nay, they might not at first be fully sensible of the moral evil of much that was tolerated or approved in pagan society. Hence in this as in other epistles, Paul is very plain and explicit in drawing the contrast between worldly and Christian living.

17. **This I say therefore, and testify in the Lord, that ye no longer**

walk as the Gentiles also walk, in the vanity of their mind,] He utters this as a solemn testimony in the Lord, *i.e.* as one abiding in Christ by faith, and speaking what he personally knows to be the mind of Christ. The word rendered "testify" is a strong and unusual one; it is not merely to declare as a matter of personal knowledge, but to protest, to make a solemn appeal as in the sight of God. It is used only on two other occasions by Paul (Acts xxvi. 22), in his solemn appeal to Agrippa in reference to his ministry as a whole; and in Gal. v. 3, "I protest again to every man that receiveth circumcision, that he is a debtor to the whole law." In reference to the gospel in general, and to two especial points in it, salvation not by law but by grace, and the indispensable necessity of holy living, Paul uses this most emphatic and solemn form of protest. "Walk," as in ver. 1, refers to their whole course of life and conduct; and when he says "no longer," he intimates that formerly their life had been such as he now solemnly warns them against. This may explain the "also," *q.d.* ye once lived a vain and ungodly life, and the Gentiles too still live so, but I call you to do so no longer. The R. V. follows the best authorities in omitting "other" before Gentiles: and this is significant. By nationality they were still Gentiles; but Paul regards them as no longer such in the religious acceptance of the term, since they were called into the body of Christ and made fellow-citizens of the saints, and of the household of God. So in 1 Cor. x. 32 he distinguishes as three great classes of mankind, "Jews, Greeks, and the Church of God."

The walk of the Gentiles is marked in general by "vanity of mind"; and the causes and consequences of that are described in vers. 18, 19. The original word, like our "mind," may denote either the mental faculty itself, or the use and application of it; and since vanity is ascribed to it, the latter is the more appropriate meaning here. "Vanity" is emptiness, unprofitableness; and so the sense is that the mind is occupied and employed about things that are perishing, and of no real worth; its exertions, however active and vigorous, lead to no solid and worthy result, and bring no satisfying good. Such a state of mind is vividly depicted in the Book of Ecclesiastes; it was very prevalent among the Greek and Roman thinkers in the apostolic age, and the presence of it is shown by the appearance of pessimism in our own day. Doubtless, however, there were then, and are now, many besides pessimistic philosophers who walk in vanity of mind, worldlings, whose thoughts and cares are engrossed with the trifles of pleasure, pride, or pelf, to the neglect of things of real and lasting value. When the apostle gives the awful picture of the walk of the Gentiles, in this and the following verses, he must be understood as speaking of what was their general character; and there is but too much evidence that this was so in his day, and is so in the heathen world still. But he does not overlook the fact that there were some who, as he says elsewhere (Rom. ii. 8), by patience in well-doing were seeking for glory and honour and incorruption, and grieving over the wickedness around them. Some such had been led to the worship of the God of Israel, like the Roman centurions and the Greeks, of whom we read in the Gospels and Acts; and more may have been groping in darkness. But such men would have been the first to confess, that on the whole the Gentile world was such as Paul has described it. After the general statement here, he goes on to trace the cause and course of this vanity; and what he says of it is very similar to his fuller description of the progress of heathen corruption in Rom. i. 18-32. The ideas and expressions are very much the same, though put in a different order and connection.

18 in the vanity of their mind; having the understanding darkened, being alienated from the life of God through the ignorance that is in them, because of the blindness of their

18. **being darkened in their understanding, alienated from the life of God because of the ignorance that is in them, because of the hardening of their heart;**] The vanity of mind in which the Gentiles walk is traced back to a twofold cause, darkness in the intellect and deadness in the moral nature; and behind these again, two other causes are mentioned, ignorance and hardening of heart. The two pairs of clauses seem to be parallel to each other, and to indicate a course of intellectual and moral corruption going on side by side, yet so that the moral degeneracy is that which lies behind the other, and to which the whole ruin is ultimately to be traced. The immediate cause of the vanity of their mind is, that they are darkened in their understanding. That is the opposite of the enlightenment for which Paul had prayed for his readers (ch. i. 18), and consists in their minds being beclouded with false notions and prejudices (comp. Rom. i. 21), which prevented them seeing the truth that was manifest even in nature. But this was not the worst of their state: they were "alienated from the life of God," *i.e.* the life that God lives in men, when they recognise that "in him we live, and move, and have our being" (Acts xvii. 28). It is not exactly the new life of regeneration that is here meant, for Paul speaks of it as a thing from which they have become alien, so that it must be something they once had, or might have had. It is that which John means when he says of the Word, through whom all things were made, "in him was life, and the life was the light of men" (John i. 4). That relation to God, in virtue of which man might do by nature the things of the law, has been broken; and now they are, as Paul had before said (ch. ii. 1), dead by trespasses and sins. Since he expressly declares this state to be one in which all men are from their birth, we must recognise a certain ideal element in the alienation here described, pointing to the one man by whom sin entered into the world and death by sin. Yet relatively it is true, that every man repeats in himself the fall of Adam, and breaks the bond of conscience that would link him to the life of God. This state of darkness and deadness is next traced back to ignorance. The clouds of error and prejudice that obfuscate the mind are due to the absence of knowledge; for if the truth were clearly known, these could not arise. But there is an abiding ignorance; the words "which is in them" are emphatic, as if to indicate, not a mere passing accident, but a habitual state. They spend their life in ignorance of God, from whose life they are alienated. But this ignorance is not such as to excuse their sin; for it is not a mere unaccountable misfortune or inevitable fate, it is due to the hardening of their heart. The heart in Scripture denotes not merely the emotions and affections, for which we generally use the word, but our whole mental and moral nature, including intellect and conscience as well. Here, however, it denotes the soul as capable of sensibility; for the word "hardening" means making callous, as the hands of labourers become by manual work, so as to be insensible to what to others would cause acute pain. It thus describes the want of susceptibility to impressions on the mind and conscience as well as the feelings, absence of awe in the presence of the divine, of shame and remorse for wrong-doing, of pity for suffering, of gratitude for kindness. Want of sensibility to such things cannot but make the soul blind to God,

19 heart: who, being past feeling, have given themselves over unto lasciviousness, to work all uncleanness with greediness. 20, 21 But ye have not so learned Christ; if so be that ye have heard him, and have been taught by him, as the truth is in

unable to understand His character, or to perceive the tokens of His being, in our own nature and in the world around us. Such callousness is an acquired thing. Paul speaks not of hardness, but of hardening. Men bring it upon themselves by disobeying the dictates of conscience and stifling its voice; and of such disobedience it is at once the natural consequence and the just punishment. It may therefore be ascribed both to man's sin, as here, and to God's just judgment, as in Rom. i. 24, 26, 28.

The next verse shows to what foul vices this state of mind and heart leads.

19. **who being past feeling gave themselves up to lasciviousness, to work** (*or* **to make a trade of**) **all uncleanness with greediness** (*or* **covetousness**).] Being past feeling, or having put away pain, expresses the result of the hardening of the heart, and that is specially connected with sensual vice, as Burns feelingly exclaims—

"But oh! it hardens a' within,
And petrifies the feeling."

Such vice is also a natural result of blindness to moral and heavenly things. As Carlyle puts it, when men are in doubt and darkness about God, freedom, and immortality, the one thing that appears certain is that they have five senses, and that these are objects that gratify them. So they give themselves to the indulgence of these: "Let us live and let us love; let us drive away cares with wine; let us eat and drink, for to-morrow we die." Such were the maxims of the heathen world among whom these Christians lived. And as sensual pleasures never can satisfy the soul made for God, they were driven from one form of sin to another, ever more vile and unnatural. So Paul may well speak of all uncleanness, or uncleanness of all kinds, as a thing they not only now and again fell into, through weakness, but practised or made a business of. The word rendered "greediness" has the same ambiguity in the original, and may either denote the greedy pursuit of sensual pleasure, or the greed of gain as another passion to which they had given themselves over. Since the phrase is literally "in greediness," and so indicates that the greed is intimately connected with the practice of uncleanness, the former view is perhaps the more probable, and the same word is used in connection with sins of sensuality in ch. v. 3 and Col. iii. 5. In any case, it indicates that sins of both kinds have a common root, in the inordinate selfishness that would grasp all for one's own enjoyment or gain.

In strong contrast to this dark picture, is now set the calling of Christians.

20, 21. **But ye did not so learn Christ; if so be that ye heard him, and were taught in him, even as truth is in Jesus:**] There is another way of rendering ver. 20, for which a good deal may be said, dividing it by a colon, so as to make it two short and abrupt sentences, "But ye *are* not so (see Luke xxii. 26): ye learned Christ." This brings out better the emphasis on the pronoun "ye"; whereas on the common view the emphatic word must be "so," which is not in an emphatic position. But the rendering of the English versions is that of the great majority of expositors, and it enables us better to see why the apostle varies the name from Christ to Jesus in ver. 21, and why he adds the conditional clause, "if so be." If Paul says, "But ye did not so learn the Christ," or the Messiah (for that is the exact rendering), he implies that there might be a way of learning Him that would not be opposed to the walk of the Gentiles. That there were professing Christians who practically lived a life of sensuality, we know from Paul's weeping testimony in Phil. iii. 18, 19. That some defended this, by a sophistical appeal to the freedom of the gospel, appears from 1 Cor. vi. 12, 13; and here we seem forced to conclude that some also taught as Christian, a religion that allowed such impurity. Of this kind seem to have been those called in Revelation Nicolaitans, or Balaamites,[1] at Ephesus (ch. ii. 6), Pergamum (ch. ii. 14), and Thyatira (ch. ii. 20-24); all of which places were probably among those to which this epistle was addressed. Thus there seems to be here a reference to false and immoral teaching, though at ver. 14 it seemed doubtful. But however such men might teach, or believe, a Messiah whose salvation would permit them to live like the heathen, Paul trusts that those to whom he writes have "learned the Christ" far otherwise. This peculiar expression, "learned the Christ," denotes not merely receiving a doctrine about Christ, but becoming acquainted with Jesus Himself. But he goes on to state the supposition on which he speaks thus: "if at least ye heard him, and were taught in him, even as truth is in Jesus." "Ye heard him" is also a peculiar expression, and seems to denote hearing His voice in the gospel that had come to them. John v. 24, 25, x. 27, have been quoted as illustrative parallels. This refers to the beginning of their Christian life, their first believing in Christ; the next clause, "were taught," to the instruction that followed upon that; both being included in "learned Christ." So in His last commission to the apostles Christ bade them "make disciples of all nations," and breaks that up into the two parts, "baptizing them . . . and teaching them . . ." (Matt. xxviii. 19, 20). The last words of this verse have been very variously understood, as their precise construction is not very clear. Although our translators and revisers have put a colon at the end of the verse, thereby disjoining from it the following clauses, it seems more natural to connect these with the verb "ye were taught," than with the remoter verbs "I say and testify" (ver. 17). Thus the main sentence would run: "if ye heard him, and were taught . . . that ye put off . . ."; and the intermediate clauses have a simple and appropriate meaning. "Ye were taught in him, that ye put off the old man," would be parallel to "proclaimed in Jesus the resurrection from the dead" (Acts iv. 2), *i.e.* by proclaiming Jesus thereby proclaimed the resurrection. So here, by being taught Christ, ye were thereby taught that ye put off the old man. This seems better than making the clause mean, "taught as being in vital union with Christ." Then the next clause comes in suitably, "even as truth is in Jesus," *i.e.* as is implied in true teaching of Jesus, the actual historical Messiah. Not without reason does Paul here use the personal name of the Saviour, instead of the official title, the Christ, which he had employed before. It is possible to teach and to learn a doctrine of the Messiah, such as was taught in the synagogue, or a theory of the Christ as an æon in Gnostic genealogies, and at the same time to indulge in licentiousness. But to hear and be taught, through what is truth in the actual Jesus of Nazareth, the pure and perfect teacher of the love of God and man, and yet to live willingly in vice, is morally impossible. Paul thus makes his appeal in defence of the pure

[1] Nicolaitan is a Greek equivalent for Balaamite in Hebrew.

22 Jesus: that ye put off concerning the former conversation the old man, which is corrupt according to the deceitful lusts;
23, 24 and be renewed in the spirit of your mind; and that ye

gospel, and against any corruption of it, to the truth in Jesus, the character and life and teaching of the historical Saviour. He is very sparing in his references to the incidents of His life on earth, of which he was not an eyewitness, and of which probably no authentic written memoir had yet been published; but he has repeatedly indicated his reverence for the character, example, and teaching of Jesus, and here we see how fundamental that was in his whole conception of Christianity.

The next verses (22–24) indicate the substance of Jesus' moral teaching, which the apostle wishes solemnly to recall to their minds.

22. that ye put away, as concerning your former manner of life, the old man, which waxeth corrupt after the lusts of deceit;] The verb "put away" is in a tense that expresses an action at a point of time not definitely specified; and here it refers to their conversion, and denotes that great initial change which Paul had before described as a quickening and raising from death in sin (ch. ii. 1–10). There he had emphasised the divine power exerted in it; here he brings out the human side of it, the conversion or turning from sin by the soul, moved and drawn by the grace of God. That is a definite putting away the old self, for that word best conveys to us the meaning of "man" in this and similar phrases in the N. T., *e.g.* "the inner man," "the hidden man of the heart." It denotes the personality, extending to every part of our nature, though viewed in each case in a special aspect. There must be an abandoning not merely of old thoughts, or old feelings, or old desires, but of what comprehends all these, the old self, the entire thinking, feeling, and acting that made up our personality. Hence the need of the qualifying clause, "as concerning your former manner of life"; for the Christian is not to lose his identity in respect of what is natural and good in his old life. In the intellect and zeal of a Paul, the generous impulsiveness of a Peter, and the like, the new man retains the features of the old; but as to the walk of the world in vanity and immorality, there is to be an entire laying aside of the old man, not merely of certain particular vices, but of the very self that lived in them. For this old self is characterised as waxing corrupt, *i.e.* being depraved in a moral sense; the man is becoming more and more unsound and rotten, in affections, in conscience, in intellect, and even, it may be, in his very physical constitution. This process is going on according to the lusts of deceit. Lusts or desires of some kind or another are all that such a man has to guide him, and they are in their own nature characterised by deceit, they lure men to the pursuit of vain glory, or uncertain riches, or pleasures that perish in the using.

Paul elsewhere refers to the same thing as here when he says, "our old man has been crucified with Christ" (Rom. vi. 6); "they that are Christ's have crucified the flesh" (Gal. v. 24): but he represents the old self, or the flesh, as still living and struggling, though it has received a deadly blow; it is nailed to the cross, but not yet quite dead. This is true to Christian experience, and hence the propriety of the exhortations here as addressed to those who are in profession Christians.

23. and that ye be renewed in the spirit of your mind,] The word rendered "be renewed" is expressive of the freshness of youth, rejuvenated,

put on the new man, which after God is created in righteousness and true holiness. Wherefore, putting away lying, in contrast with the decaying and perishing of the old self according to the lusts of deceit. And the form of the verb indicates that it is a gradual process, not done at one stroke, but continually going on. The phrase "the spirit of your mind" is a peculiar one, not found elsewhere in the N. T., and therefore its exact meaning is open to question. Many understand by it the Holy Spirit of God as dwelling and working in the mind of the believer, and would render the clause "by the Spirit" that you have received through Christ, and that now rules your mind. Some countenance is given to this interpretation by the fact that, in Rom. vii. 23, Paul speaks of the "law of his mind" as opposed to the "law of sin in his members," and calls it also "the law of the Spirit of life" (Rom. viii. 2). But others think that it is the human soul that is meant, and that Paul means that the governing principle of man, even in his higher intellectual life, needs to be renovated. The former interpretation, however, gives a more definite and pointed meaning. Instead of the vanity of mind in which the heathen walk, the Christian has his mind so animated by the Spirit of God that he is gradually made more and more fresh or youthful, being filled with the strength of new and vigorous life giving zest and interest to all his thoughts and mental occupations.

24. **and put on the new man, which after God hath been created (*or which is after God created*) in righteousness and holiness of truth.**] The new man is not Christ, although the expression "put on Christ" is used by Paul in Rom. xiii. 14 and Gal. iii. 27; yet here the contrast with "the old man" shows that it is to be understood rather as the new self or character. When this new self is said to have been created, the meaning may be either, like the expression in ch. ii. 10, "good works which God afore prepared," that the pattern or ideal of renewed life was called into being by God in Christ, or that by the regeneration of each Christian there is created in him a new life, and that his subsequent progress in holiness consists in identifying his will more and more with it, walking not after the flesh, but after the Spirit. Whichever be the precise meaning, Paul gives us the encouraging assurance that the new character we are to aim at is wrought by God's power, and will conform us to God's likeness. "After God" means, as the parallel passage in Col. iii. 10 shows, after God's image; and there is a manifest allusion to Gen. i. 26, 27, where God is said to have made man in His image, after His likeness. The new creation in Christ restores and perfects the old. The resemblance that we are to aim at consists in righteousness and holiness of truth. Righteousness is the quality that inclines to the fulfilment of all the duties of equal love to our fellows; "holiness" is not here the comprehensive term denoting heart consecration to God, in view of which believers are called saints or holy ones; it is rather "piety," in that old sense of the term, that included not only godliness, but dutiful affection to parents and kindred. But it is defined as piety of truth, or of the truth, so as to indicate that it is not the mere feeling that may arise from instinct or habit, but the affection that is rooted in the knowledge of the true relations of God and man.

The general exhortation contained in this paragraph (vers. 17–24) is now applied in detail to some of the more ordinary and needful cases in common life. Paul shows himself here intensely practical, and will leave his readers no room for doubt what vices he would have them to abandon, and what virtues they must cultivate.

speak every man truth with his neighbour: for we are
26 members one of another. Be ye angry, and sin not: let not
27 the sun go down upon your wrath: neither give place to

25. Wherefore, putting away falsehood, speak ye truth each one with
his neighbour: for we are members one of another.] Absolute regard for
truth is one of the most striking points in which Christian ethics are distinguished from those of heathenism; and the first inference that Paul draws,
from the general duty of putting off the old man and putting on the new, is
the call to put away falsehood, and speak truth. Falsehood is more comprehensive than "lying," for it includes not only speaking a known untruth,
but every kind of false pretence or appearance. These are to be put away
as part of the old man. The positive part of this precept is taken almost
verbally from the LXX. of Zech. viii. 16, with only a slight change which
makes it agree more exactly with the original Hebrew. The Greek translators
had rendered "every man to his neighbour"; but the closeness of association
is better brought out by the more accurate "with his neighbour." Paul,
however, does not formally quote the passage, as he had previously cited Ps.
lxviii. 18; but only uses its language, showing how familiar to his mind were
the very words of the O. T., both in the original and in the Greek translation.
He adds a reason for this duty, "for we are members one of another."
Members of the same body should be governed by the same mind; but this
they cannot be if one misrepresents or disguises anything to another. They
must know each other as they really are, if they are to act together as one
body. Truth is not merely a duty of charity to individuals, but of obligation
to the common good. To deceive men for their own advantage, though it
may not be to injure them, is not to treat them as those who, along with us,
are members one of another, but as being inferior in nature. So Paul had
already (ver. 15) spoken of doing truth in love, as the means by which the
body of Christ is built up and grows to its full stature. Thus the duty of
truth is put upon a truly Christian basis, as it is also in the parallel passage
in Col. iii. 9.

26, 27. Be ye angry, and sin not: let not the sun go down upon your
wrath: neither give place to the devil.] Here again Paul uses words of
the O. T. exactly as they are given in the LXX. and in the margin of the
R. V. of Ps. iv. 4, though in the text both the A. V. and the R. V.
translate "stand in awe." Since the apostle does not quote them as a proof,
it is of no importance, for the understanding of his meaning, whether of the
two translations best expresses the thought of the Psalmist; but it is worthy
of notice that in the Psalm the words follow a warning against falsehood
(ver. 2), and a reference to the godliness (ver. 3), of which Paul had just
spoken (ver. 24). The connection in Paul's mind may have been, that
truthfulness may often require the frank expression of disapproval and indignation, which if unrestrained is a copious source of sin. In worldly
society, smooth relations are often kept up by conventional forms of falsehood,
which are inconsistent with Christian truthfulness. In the absence of these
among those who, as Christians, are members one of another, concord must
be maintained by deeper principles.

The imperative is not merely permissive or hypothetical, as if it meant
"you may be angry," or "if you are angry"; rather it indicates that anger
may sometimes be a duty. Anger at what is wrong, at men who are false,

28 the devil. Let him that stole steal no more: but rather let him labour, working with *his* hands the thing which is good, 29 that he may have to give to him that needeth. Let no cor-

ungodly, cruel, is God-like; for His wrath comes on the children of disobedience; and Christ-like, for He looked upon hard-hearted hypocrites with anger (Mark iii. 5); and a character incapable of such feeling would not be the Christian ideal. So the apostle says, "Be ye angry." As you speak truth, and put away all the pleasant fashions, in which men call evil good and put sweet for bitter, you will and should feel and express righteous indignation at sin. But let your anger be sinless in its nature, and short in its duration. It will be without sin, if, like the anger of God and of Christ, it is always joined with love and pity. So when Christ looked round on the scribes with anger, He was also moved with pity; and that very world against which God's wrath is revealed, He so loved as to give His only-begotten Son to save. That your wrath may also be short, let fading sunlight admonish you. If you have had just occasion during the day for an outburst of anger, that is the meaning of "wrath" in the end of the verse, let not the sun set while it is still hot in you. If you would, like the Psalmist, lie down in peace and sleep (Ps. iv. 8), see that you do it, as much as in you lies, at peace with all men.

The following admonition, "neither give place to the devil," warns us that our great spiritual adversary may gain an advantage over us if we indulge sinful or persistent anger. For, though some have thought that the word we render "devil" may have been meant here in its literal sense of "slanderer," that is very unlikely, since wherever Paul uses the word with the definite article he means Satan. The reason for a reference to him in this connection seems to be, the danger to the Christian community as a whole. In 2 Cor. ii. 11, Paul warns against too great severity in dealing with a fallen brother, by this consideration, "that no advantage may be gained over us by Satan." Anything that interrupts the unity and concord that should prevail among the brethren, opens a breach into which our watchful and cunning enemy is ever ready to rush in.

28. **Let him that stole steal no more: but rather let him labour, working with his hands the thing that is good, that he may have whereof to give to him that needeth.**] Here Paul uses very plain language, giving its true name to all dishonesty. He speaks of this as possibly existing among his readers. For the word rendered "stole" is literally "steals." It is not merely an admonition to one who has been formerly a thief, but has ceased to be so, not to relapse into his old practice; but it is a call to any who may be even yet guilty of it, to abandon the sin. The gospel has a message, alike of warning and encouragement, to all sinners; and as the apostle doubtless includes in stealing every way of obtaining unjustly what is not one's own, there may have been, even among Christian converts in those days, some who were guilty of that sin. Can it be said that this is not the case even yet? The exhortation, therefore, is not needless or inappropriate. Like Christ and all His disciples, Paul is not content with inculcating abstinence from positive wrong, he sets over against it the good that we should do. The need and desire of earthly possessions, that is abused when allowed to be a motive to steal, finds its legitimate satisfaction in honest work, that produces something of use. This is the God-appointed way of providing for one's needs, and it

rupt communication proceed out of your mouth, but that which is good to the use of edifying, that it may minister grace 30 unto the hearers. And grieve not the Holy Spirit of God, 31 whereby ye are sealed unto the day of redemption. Let all

enables us not only not to deprive anyone of what is his, but actually to give to those who have not. The word is literally "to communicate," or share with him that has need; and this expression shows the true nature and blessing of Christian giving. It is not really parting with what we have wrought for, it is enjoying it through others, getting more real happiness out of it than either the miser who hoards, or the spendthrift who wastes it, when we partake of it with others. Thus a truly Christian motive is connected with the homely duty of industrious work for a living.

29. **Let no corrupt speech proceed out of your mouth, but such as is good for edifying as the need may be** (*Gr.* **the building up of the need), that it may give grace to them that hear.**] From a warning against injuring others by dishonest deeds, Paul proceeds to one against doing so by corrupt speech; for the positive good that he contrasts with the forbidden evil shows that corrupt speech is viewed as doing harm to the hearers. "Corrupt" is literally rotten; but it is used in a more general sense, when Jesus speaks of a corrupt tree bringing forth evil fruit (Matt. vii. 17), for noxious or bad in general. Here Paul condemns any use of the faculty of speech, that is morally unhealthy in its character or tendency, that expresses or suggests impure feelings, light views of sin, irreverence towards God, or trifling with serious things. Some special forms of such corrupt speech are mentioned further on (ver. 31, ch. v. 4); here the apostle forbids in general all speech that is morally injurious, and urges, as the only way to avoid this, that we make our speaking truly useful in the highest and best way. Instead of corrupting or breaking down anything good, we should aim at edifying or building up, *i.e.* helping those who hear to build up their character into likeness to Christ. This is to be done with reference to the need of the occasion when we speak, and that may be various from time to time. It may be instruction, or counsel, or warning, or sympathy in sorrow, or relieving the strain of work and worry by seasonable and innocent mirth. In such ways, Christians, by their daily common conversation, should seek "to give grace to those that hear." By grace is not meant here the favour of God, but simply kindness or good done by us. So Paul uses the word in 2 Cor. i. 15 ("that ye might have a second benefit"), and so here he simply means that you may do some good.

30. **And grieve not the Holy Spirit of God, in whom ye were sealed unto the day of redemption.**] As he had enforced his former precept, against sinful wrath, by a reference to our danger from our great spiritual enemy (ver. 27), so Paul enforces this, by reminding us of our divine Sanctifier. The Spirit of God shows His working in men specially by the gifts of utterance that He bestows: prophecy, speaking with tongues, witness-bearing for Christ, are gifts of the Spirit specially abundant in the apostolic age, and though some have passed away, the gifts of wisdom and exhortation and spiritual song have been perennial in the Church. The Spirit that bestows these is the Holy Spirit, as He is most emphatically called here; and what can be conceived more abhorrent to Him, than that corrupt speech should proceed out of mouths into which He has put such gifts of utterance? Since

bitterness, and wrath, and anger, and clamour, and evil
32 speaking, be put away from you, with all malice: and be ye
kind one to another, tender-hearted, forgiving one another,
even as God for Christ's sake hath forgiven you.
CHAP. V. 1. Be ye therefore followers of God, as dear children;

He is here said to be grieved, it appears that Paul looked upon the Spirit of God as personal; for he cannot mean merely the holy and spiritual God, as when it is said "his soul was grieved" (Judg. x. 16), since the Holy Spirit is spoken of as having a special relation to believers. In Him, he says, ye were sealed unto the day of redemption, using the same figure as before in ch. i. 13, only there he describes it as "by," here as "in," the Holy Spirit. Perhaps the variation of expression has no intended significance; but, strictly taken, the idea here is that we are compassed about by the Holy Spirit, taken into His embrace as it were, and so stamped with the likeness of God. The day of redemption is that on which Christ shall come to claim and take possession of those whom He has bought with His blood, and marked with His Spirit, while they are in the world and not yet finally delivered from its evil.

31, 32. Let all bitterness, and wrath, and anger, and clamour, and railing, be put away from you, with all malice; and be ye kind one to another, tender-hearted, forgiving each other, even as God also in Christ forgave you.] Here again there is first a dissuasive from evil, and then an exhortation to the opposite good. The evil is ill-feeling one to another, showing itself in passion, whether as a sudden, violent outburst, or as a lingering animosity; for that seems to be the difference between wrath and anger; then in clamour, such as brawling or scolding; and in railing, slandering or traducing in any way. With these various forms and phases of bad temper is joined "all malice," the more general expression for malevolent affections. These are all to be put away; and the way in which this is to be done is by cultivating the opposite graces, looking to the example of God in Christ. We are to be to one another, kind, that is the opposite of all malice, and more particularly tender-hearted, *i.e.* full of feeling, easily touched and moved by another's woe. This will make it easier for us to be forgiving. The word here used for that is a very strong one, freely forgiving or giving grace. No doubt it refers chiefly to the way of dealing with offences, which are apt to provoke anger, clamour, and railing; but it is more general, and includes any sort of gracious gift, the giving up of one's rights to another, or the extending of help and benefit to him. "Each other" in the R. V. represents a different and stronger word than "one another" in the previous clause; literally, it is "yourselves," the idea being that Christians should feel so much one, that an act of kindness or forgiveness to a brother is really done to oneself. For this Paul sets before us the very highest pattern and motive, "as God in Christ forgave you." The A. V. "for Christ's sake" is not quite correct, though certainly it is true. The thought here is a more comprehensive one: God is the author of the forgiveness of sins; it comes from Him as a free gift of pure grace; He bestows it in Christ, by giving Him to be the propitiation for our sins. If we have received such a grace, that cost God so much and costs us nothing, shall we not strive to exercise the like grace to our fellows? It is the lesson that Jesus taught in the parable of the unmerciful servant (Matt. xviii. 15–35), which Paul perhaps knew, and remembered here.

V. 1. Be ye therefore imitators of God, as beloved children;] This

2 and walk in love, as Christ also hath loved us, and hath given himself for us an offering and a sacrifice to God for a

exhortation follows the preceding naturally and without break. It is the application of the foregoing injunction to forbearance and forgiveness; for it is in these qualities especially that we are here called to be like God ; and the motive and encouragement is, that we are, and will thus show ourselves to be, children of God and objects of His love. The precept and the reason given are exactly the same as in the words of Jesus, as recorded both by Matthew (v. 45–48) and Luke (vi. 35, 36); and it is difficult to doubt that Paul was acquainted with these sayings of the Master, from oral reports, if not from written records.

2. **and walk in love, even as Christ also loved you, and gave himself up for us (*or* you), an offering and a sacrifice to God for an odour of a sweet smell.**] This precept, too, is from the teaching of Jesus Himself, in its general idea contained in all the Gospels, but in its exact form in that of John (xiii. 34), "A new commandment I give unto you, That ye love one another ; even as I have loved you, that ye also love one another :" and (xv. 12, 13), "This is my commandment, That ye love one another, even as I have loved you. Greater love hath no man than this, that a man lay down his life for his friends." In the very same way Paul mentions here Christ's giving Himself up as the great work and proof of His love. According to the text followed by the revisers, the apostle here changes from the second person ("you") to the first ("us"); but there is considerable uncertainty about the pronoun here and in ch. iv. 32, as can easily be understood. The use of the second person proceeds from the earnestness of the address ; but Paul cannot recall Christ's love and sacrifice without remembering that he as well as his readers is included in it, and rests his hopes upon it. Nor can he mention the work of Christ as our example, without saying, though only in a passing clause, that it is much more. So also Peter (1 Pet. ii. 21–25), showing that to the apostles the example of love, while a real end of Christ's death, was not its chief, much less its only purpose. We need not, however, in this place give the preposition "for" any more than the general meaning "for our good," though in some places the context shows that it is equivalent to "instead of." But Paul undoubtedly views Christ's giving Himself up as being a sacrifice, as Jesus' own words imply, when He called His blood that of the covenant shed for many. Paul has in his view the words of Lev. i. 9, and perhaps also of Ps. xl. 6 and Ezek. xx. 41 ; and his meaning undoubtedly is that Christ gave Himself up to God, in His life and especially in His death, and that His entire surrender of Himself was well pleasing to God. The expression "a savour of a sweet smell" is plainly a figurative one, perhaps originally transferred from the rude notions of the Deity as like a magnified man, that prevailed in early times. But even the Jews knew that what really pleased God was not the burning of incense and lambs on the altar, but the devotion and gratitude which that expressed. So what was pleasing to God in the sacrifice of Christ was, not the suffering and death as such, but the love and patience and holiness with which these were endured. The emphasising of the fact, that Christ's sacrifice was not only an act of love to man, but also of obedience, devotion, childlike love to God, serves to show that the love in which we are called to walk should be of this character also, that it should not be of the nature of earthly passion, or easy good-nature only, but a heavenly affection, that always looks to God, and seeks to bring others to God also. Thus the transition is not unnatural

3 sweet-smelling savour. But fornication, and all uncleanness, or covetousness, let it not be once named among you, as 4 becometh saints; neither filthiness, nor foolish talking, nor jesting, which are not convenient: but rather giving of thanks. 5 For this ye know, that no whoremonger, nor unclean person, nor covetous man, who is an idolater, hath any inheritance 6 in the kingdom of Christ and of God. Let no man deceive

to those forms of impurity that are referred to with so startling an abruptness in the next verse.

3, 4. But fornication, and all uncleanness, or covetousness, let it not even be named among you, as becometh saints; nor filthiness, nor foolish talking, or jesting, which are not befitting: but rather giving of thanks.] These are forms of evil into which the social affections of men are apt to run, corruptions and impurities attaching to the good fellowship and boon companionship of ungodly men; as the sins against which he had given warning in ch. iv. 25-31 were for the most part outflowings of the selfish or angry passions. In the former paragraph Paul had been illustrating the righteousness in which the new man is created: here he illustrates its godliness of truth. That it should be necessary to warn Christians against such gross sensual vices, will surprise no one who knows how these prevailed, and with what indifference they were regarded in the heathen society of that day, as indeed is the case in heathen countries still. On the connection of covetousness or greediness with such vices, see above on ch. iv. 19. The word rendered "jesting" is one generally used in secular writers for a quality to be admired, "facetiousness"; and perhaps Paul introduces it here as a fair name given to foolish talking, as if he said, "or what is called facetiousness." For the admired wit of the cleverest comic writers both of ancient and modern times often raises laughter at the expense of decency; and one of the avenues to impurity is the delight in such facetiousness. The expression of disapproval is better given in the R. V. by changing "convenient" into "befitting"; and it is weighty by its moderate and negative form. For saints, *i.e.* those whom God has chosen and taken to be His own people, what is becoming, as an expression of mirth and social happiness, is not any such unhallowed jesting, but rather giving of thanks, joyful praise to God for His good gifts, and a temperate and pure-hearted enjoyment of them.

5. For this ye know of a surety, that no fornicator, nor unclean person, nor covetous man, which is an idolater, hath any inheritance in the kingdom of Christ and God.] Here Paul asserts as the ground of his emphatic command, a solemn truth, as to which he appeals to their own knowledge, or bids them know, for possibly the verb should be taken as an imperative. The words "of a surety" represent the participle of another verb, and might be literally rendered "being aware." What he thus asserts is, that none guilty of the sins he has mentioned has any part in Christ's kingdom, and he repeats the worst forms of these sins, with the additional reminder, that every covetous man is an idolater: wealth, or, as Jesus calls it, Mammon, the god of wealth, being then the chief object of love and reverence that was a rival to the living God. "Inheritance" means lot assigned, and in this case it is a part in the blessing enjoyed in the divine kingdom. It is not certain whether that kingdom is conceived by Paul here as a thing of the future, or as already present. In the former part of the epistle he had spoken

you with vain words: for because of these things cometh the
wrath of God upon the children of disobedience. Be not ye
therefore partakers with them. For ye were sometimes darkness, but now *are ye* light in the Lord: walk as children of
light; (for the fruit of the Spirit *is* in all goodness, and right-

of Christ as exalted to the right hand of God, and having all things put under
His feet (ch. i. 20–22), and of believers as raised with Him (ch. ii. 6), and
blessed in Him with all spiritual blessings in the heavenlies (ch. i. 3). But
he had also spoken of a redemption that is still future (chs. i. 14, iv. 30), when
the Lord shall take actual possession of the people He has purchased and
sealed for Himself, and when they shall have, not only the earnest, but the
full enjoyment of the inheritance. It is most natural to refer the statement
here to that blessed consummation to which the hopes of Christians are
directed. The kingdom is said to be "of Christ and God." By strict
grammatical rule, the phrase means one person, "him who is Christ and
God"; and it is consistent with Paul's general conception of Christ that he
should apply the name God to Him, as he has almost certainly done in
Rom. ix. 5. But in a passage coming so soon after the distinct mention of
Christ and God in ver. 2, it is perhaps more probable that he did not mean
the phrase in its precise grammatical sense, but intended to mention our Lord
Jesus and God distinctly. Even so, however, he associates them so closely,
ascribing one and the same kingdom to both, that we cannot doubt that he
believed and taught the true Deity of our Saviour.

6. **Let no man deceive you with empty words: for because of these
things cometh the wrath of God upon the sons of disobedience.**] Paul
would have them not only be fully aware of the inconsistency of such conduct
with any part in the kingdom of God, but be on their guard against any
arguments, however plausible, by which any might lead them to think lightly
of them. He evidently knew that there were many who might do so, both
heathens, whose code of morals did not severely condemn such vices, and
professing Christians, who perverted his teaching, about the grace of God and
the believer's freedom from the law, to a cloak of licentiousness. Against all
such hollow and empty reasonings he sets the solemn truth, that it is on
account of these things that God's anger comes on the disobedient. The
verb is in the present tense, but from its meaning may include a reference to
the future also. The holy indignation of the Judge of all is already, and shall
be more plainly and terribly at the last, against those who will not allow
themselves to be persuaded to turn to God and accept His mercy; but it comes
on them, not merely because they do not believe God's word, but because of
their offences against His law of purity and holiness. Hence Paul continues:

7. **Be not ye therefore partakers with them:**] Ye would not share with
them in that terrible doom; see, then, that you are not induced in any way
to take part with them in those sins that bring it on them. Thus the very
neighbourhood of those who practised or tolerated such evils is skilfully made
an additional reason for avoiding them; and this all the more, because they
had themselves once lived in the same state of blindness and ignorance, in
which the heathen around them still are.

8, 9, 10. **for ye were once darkness, but are now light in the Lord:
walk as children of light (for the fruit of the light is in all goodness and
righteousness and truth¹ proving what is well-pleasing unto the Lord;**]

10 eousness, and truth;) proving what is acceptable unto the
11 Lord. And have no fellowship with the unfruitful works of
12 darkness, but rather reprove *them*. For it is a shame even
to speak of those things which are done of them in secret.

This is the last reference that Paul makes in this epistle to the recent conversion of his readers; and as he had reminded them of it, first, that they might value their Christian privileges and blessings (ch. ii. 1, 11), and then that they might live a holy life (ch. iv. 17), he now recurs to it with a view to their having an influence for good on those around them. Hence he uses the figure of darkness for the heathen world, with which the light in the Lord is contrasted. The expression is very strong, "ye were once, not merely in the dark, but darkness itself." But that is no longer your state: now ye are light, since ye are in the Lord, who has come into the world to be the light of the world. Then, he continues, walk as children of light, proving what is well-pleasing to the Lord. This is the connection of the clauses, ver. 9 being an explanatory parenthesis. You are in the Lord, *i.e.* the Lord Jesus, who is your light; and so you see clearly what is well-pleasing to Him; hence you will make proof of that by doing it, and so commend it to others. The same idea of proving by trial the will of God is expressed by Paul in Rom. xii. 2. "that ye may prove what is the good and acceptable and perfect will of God." The parenthetic ver. 9 explains what this is. "The fruit of the light" is the reading preferred by the revisers and all scholars to "the fruit of the Spirit"; and it keeps up the figure and connection. The things that come from being light in the Lord are goodness, *i.e.* kindness or benevolence; righteousness, *i.e.* equal love and regard to our fellows, and truth. These distinguish the children of light, and show what is well-pleasing to the Lord. In contrast with these are the works of darkness.

11, 12. **and have no fellowship with the unfruitful works of darkness, but rather even reprove (or convict) them; for the things which are done by them in secret it is a shame even to speak of.**] In order to show that the productions of light are substantial, living, and useful, while those of darkness are perishable and useless, he calls the one "fruit," *i.e.* the growth of vital power with life and seed in it; while the other he describes as unfruitful works, deeds that have no permanent benefit, enjoyments that perish in the using. In the same way in Gal. v. 19, 22, he speaks of the "works" of the flesh on the one hand, but of the "fruit" of the Spirit on the other; and in Rom. vi. 21 he asks, "What fruit had ye at that time in the things whereof ye are now ashamed?" implying that they derived no real and lasting good from them; and then goes on, "But now . . . ye have your fruit unto holiness, and the end everlasting life." Here too, as there, the unfruitful works are things to be ashamed of. The Asian converts are living among those who do in secret such works of darkness as it is a shame even to speak of; and Paul would have them see that they be not drawn into any complicity with them. The best security against this is, not merely a negative standing aloof, but a positive reproof or conviction of them. The word denotes not mere denunciation, but a convincing exposition of the evil of such deeds; it answers to the proving what is well-pleasing to the Lord. That naturally implies a reproving of what is the opposite. Let your walk as children of light be such as to show something of what goodness is, and so also by contrast how shameful are the works of darkness. The idea is like that

13 But all things that are reproved are made manifest by the
14 light: for whatsoever doth make manifest is light. Wherefore he saith, Awake thou that sleepest, and arise from the
15 dead, and Christ shall give thee light. See then that ye walk

expressed by Milton, when he represents a holy angel encountering Satan—

> "And his grave rebuke,
> Severe in youthful beauty, added grace
> Invincible; abashed the devil stood,
> And felt how awful goodness is, and saw
> Virtue in her shape how lovely; saw
> And pined his loss."—*Paradise Lost*, iv. 844-49.

But the conviction of which Paul speaks here is not to lead to a hopeless pining their loss, but by God's grace to a blessed enlightenment and conversion. For he goes on to say :

13. **But all things when they are reproved (*or* convicted) are made manifest by the light: for everything that is made manifest is light.**] By "all things" are meant especially all the things he is speaking of, the unfruitful works of darkness. These, when convicted by the faithful word and consistent walk of those who were once darkness but now are light in the Lord, are made manifest; and when this is really done, and men are willing to have their evil deeds brought to the light, they are themselves also made light. For Paul adds, "everything that is made manifest is light." There is no doubt that the revisers were right in changing the active "doth make" into the passive, for the form is the same as in the preceding clause, and it always has a passive meaning in N. T. This also agrees better with the context, for it appears from the following verse, that Paul is showing how the reproof of the children of light may lead to the conversion of those who are still in darkness. The idea that being brought to the light is the one thing needful, is strikingly parallel to that contained in Jesus' words in John iii. 19-21. It must be remembered that in both passages the light is not mere knowledge or moral teaching, but salvation brought by Christ and reflected by His followers.

14. **Wherefore he saith, Awake, thou that sleepest, and arise from the dead, and Christ shall shine upon thee.**] This is a quotation adduced to confirm or illustrate what has just been said ; and it is introduced in a way in which the N. T. writers in general bring in citations from O. T. Scripture. "He" is indefinite, and is to be understood as meaning God, or the Scripture, or the Holy Spirit, which are used as equivalent. But the words are not a literal rendering of any O. T. passage ; and some have thought they may have been taken from some prophecy now lost, or from a Christian hymn. It is, however, more probable that they are a free paraphrase of Isa. lx. 1, 2 : "Arise, shine ; for thy light is come, and the glory of the Lord is risen upon thee. For, behold, darkness shall cover the earth, and gross darkness the peoples ; but the Lord shall arise upon thee, and his glory shall be seen upon thee." The words of the prophet are addressed to Israel in a time of religious declension and death, described in ch. lix.; and they are a call to rise from that torpor, and meet the light of Jehovah's glory, which will make them a light to the heathen who are in darkness around them. Thus they convey the same idea that Paul has been presenting, and in the individual and Christian form into which he has cast them, they come as a rousing call to those who may be giving way to sleep, stimulating and encouraging them to be

16 circumspectly, not as fools, but as wise, redeeming the time,
17 because the days are evil. Wherefore be ye not unwise, but
18 understanding what the will of the Lord *is*. And be not drunk
with wine, wherein is excess; but be filled with the Spirit;
19 speaking to yourselves in psalms, and hymns, and spiritual

up and doing, so as to receive the light of Christ, and spread it abroad among those dying in darkness. But I am inclined on the whole to think that the facts adduced by Resch, referred to in the Introduction above, make it most probable that Paul is here citing a saying of Jesus that has not been recorded in the Gospels.

15, 16. **Look therefore carefully how ye walk, not as unwise, but as wise; redeeming the time** (*Gr.* buying up the opportunity), **for the days are evil.**] Here Paul resumes the exhortation about the walk of the children of light (ver. 8), and defines it more exactly by pointing out the wisdom needed for it. He had spoken of the purity that becomes such; and after showing what the blessed effect of that might be, he draws from this consideration the inference, that they should have, not only the moral abhorrence of evil, but Christian wisdom, to guide their conduct carefully, so that it might conduce to the end in view. For wisdom acts in the way of adapting means to ends; and one special exercise of this is to seize every opportunity of furthering the object in view, even though at the cost of giving up something else that might in itself be desirable and good. This is what is meant by redeeming the opportunity, buying up, by some sacrifice of our own pleasure or profit, the opportunity of bringing light to those around. This applies to each particular occasion of doing good that may present itself to us, and also to the whole of our lifetime, as a precious opportunity, the day of grace, in which the Saviour offers Himself to us and to all men to be the light of our life. All the more forcible is this injunction, because of what is added, "the days are evil." They are so because of the evil that is done in them. Well might the apostle say this from his prison in Rome, amid all the rampant wickedness and widespread suffering of the days of Nero. The wonderful thing is, that in his situation he refers to the evils of the times only in this one brief clause, and that his letter is so pervaded with joy, thankfulness, and hope. Yet this one reference shows that he was not insensible of the terrible prevalence of sin and sorrow, and the discouragements even of the Christian cause.

17. **Wherefore be ye not foolish, but understand what the will of the Lord is.**] This repeats in a stronger form the need of wisdom, and shows how it is to be gained. It is, literally, "be not void of mind," senseless, as you will be apt to become by careless conduct. And if any ask, how is such wisdom as has been described to be attained? the last clause shows that it is by understanding, comprehending or taking in, what the will of the Lord is. If we give heed to the word of God, and especially to the teaching and example of the Lord Jesus Christ, we shall have the true, practical, and spiritual wisdom to guide us in a holy life. In contrast with this, Paul goes on to give a warning against a way in which men often seek to cheer themselves and others, when they feel that the days are evil, but which most surely leads to folly and senselessness.

18, 19. **And be not drunken with wine, wherein is riot, but be filled with the Spirit** (*or* **in spirit**); **speaking one to another** (*or* **to yourselves**)

songs, singing and making melody in your heart to the Lord;

in psalms and hymns and spiritual songs, singing and making melody with your heart to the Lord;] The first clause of ver. 18 is, like several of the preceding exhortations, taken verbally from the Greek version of O. T., being given by the LXX. at Prov. xxiii. 30, though the clause is not in the Hebrew text. It is not quoted here as an authority, but simply used to clothe the precept in familiar and sacred language. That the warning was, and still is, needful for professing, and even real, Christians, is but too certain. "Riot" is a more adequate word than "excess" (A. V.), and reminds us of the use of the same word in the parable of the Prodigal, who "wasted his substance with riotous living" (Luke xv. 13). But the original is even stronger, ruin, utter loss, of substance, of body, and of soul. "In which" refers to the whole clause, being drunken with wine. But the contrast which the apostle goes on to set against this is very striking, and even startling. For he presents, as the opposite alternative to the intoxication of drink, the holy state of being filled with or in the Spirit of God. Worldly men seek exhilaration in stimulants that lead to drunkenness and ruin; but Christians may have an exhilaration, safe, holy, and heavenly in its character, in the influence of the Spirit. The peculiar phrase in the original, "filled in Spirit," was perhaps used to indicate that the Spirit is not only an influence within us, but an infinite Being, in whom we are.

It is the social aspect of this spiritual exhilaration that Paul has chiefly in view; and in ver. 19 he develops this, with a tacit contrast to the feasts and revels of the world. But the clauses, as commonly punctuated, do not run very naturally. In psalms and hymns men do not speak to one another, but to God; and to give the words "to yourselves" the meaning "alternately with one another," is rather forced. Further, psalms, hymns, and songs are more naturally connected with singing than with speaking. A different division of clauses removes these incongruities thus: "be filled with the Spirit speaking to one another; in psalms and hymns and spiritual songs singing; and making melody in your heart to the Lord." Thus there would be a reference, first, to the conversation of Christians as pervaded by the influence of the Spirit, then to the expression of their feelings in song, and then to the melody of the heart with which it is accompanied. The reference is not exclusively to meetings for worship, but to Christian social meetings in general; and the materials of song are described as three: psalms, *i.e.* probably those of the O. T.; hymns, a word denoting an utterance of praise to God, and applied to some of the Psalms in their Greek titles, but here probably meaning additional compositions of that kind, such as were very early composed and sung by Christians; and songs, which is a more general term, and therefore is qualified by the adjective "spiritual," *i.e.* religious or Christian in their character, as contrasted with the worldly and profane. The name song is also applied to many of the Psalms; but as they are all comprehended in the first name, others are probably meant, differing from hymns in not being directly addressed to God. The word rendered "making melody" properly means playing, except when it is used for "singing psalms," which it cannot mean here. But it is used figuratively; for "in your heart" cannot mean merely "heartily," it indicates that the melody that accompanies the Christian songs should be that of a heart full of the sentiments expressed in them. Thus the whole passage presents the spiritual counterpart of worldly revelry, in which jesting and wine and song and music

20 giving thanks always for all things unto God and the Father
21 in the name of our Lord Jesus Christ; submitting yourselves
22 one to another in the fear of God. Wives, submit yourselves

are the sources of enjoyment. And the following verses complete the picture, and make it more general.

20, 21. giving thanks always for all things in the name of our Lord Jesus Christ to God, even the Father (*Gr.* the God and Father); subjecting yourselves one to another in the fear of Christ.] After what he had written before in this epistle of how God has blessed us with all spiritual blessings in Christ, Paul did not need to explain how Christians can give thanks to God always for all things; but he mentions this as a duty, the discharge of which will greatly promote their happiness. And as all the blessings that we daily receive come to us from Him, who is both our God and our Father through Jesus Christ our Lord, so our thanks should go up to Him in that gracious character, in the name of Christ, *i.e.* having access to God only through Christ, and believing that our thanksgiving as well as our prayers will be well-pleasing to God for Christ's sake. With gratitude to God is closely connected another element in the social exhilaration of Christians, that of mutual subjection. The riot and intoxication of worldly feasts lead to quarrels and brawls; the pure and thankful delight of spiritual exhilaration tends to concord, if we remember this precept. In whatever way anyone can help or profit a brother, he is in that to be subject to him; and as our gifts and powers are different, every one may be so in some respect. "The eye cannot say to the hand, I have no need of thee: nor the head to the feet, I have no need of you" (1 Cor. xii. 21). One may minister to another in spiritual things, as by teaching or admonition, while the other may return the service in temporal things. Each is to use his special gift for service, and so there will be a unity and harmony among all. This is to be done in the fear of Christ, for so undoubtedly we ought to read instead of "God" as in A. V. The fear meant is not slavish terror, but reverence, as for Him who is our supreme Lord and Head, whom we are afraid to displease. And Christ is most appropriately mentioned here; for this was a most essential and characteristic part of His teaching, that His kingdom was not to be like those of this world, in which the great ones exercised authority over their fellows. "But whosoever would become great among you, shall be your minister: and whosoever would be first among you shall be servant of all: even as the Son of man came not to be ministered unto, but to minister, and to give his life a ransom for many" (Mark x. 43-45). Thus here, as throughout, Paul shows his acquaintance with and following of the teaching of his Master.

V. 22–VI. 9. *Exhortation to mutual subjection.*—This is illustrated in its application to the various relations of domestic life, those of wives and husbands (vers. 22-33), children and parents (ch. vi. 1-4), servants and masters (ch. vi. 5-9); not as if these were the only relations to which it applies, but as the most natural and universal, and as specimens of its application to others, such as scholars and teachers, subjects and rulers, people and pastors, and the like. In each of the cases he mentions, he addresses first the inferior side of the relation, to whom the duty of submission most directly and obviously applies; and then shows how a corresponding subjection is due on the other side also.

22. Wives, *be in subjection* unto your own husbands, as unto the Lord.]

23 unto your own husbands, as unto the Lord. For the husband
is the head of the wife, even as Christ is the head of the
24 church: and he is the saviour of the body. Therefore, as the
church is subject unto Christ, so *let* the wives *be* to their own

Probably the verb rendered "be in subjection" should be omitted, as not being in the oldest copies of the original, the meaning being supplied from the previous verse, "subjecting yourselves"; and hence we see that it is not a passive state, but a free and voluntary act and habit that is meant, and one that is common to all Christians, and to be done by all to one another. Thus it is seen that the last clause of this verse does not imply that the husband's authority is as absolute as that of our Lord, but rather that this, like all other Christian duties, is to be done as to Christ. When we do any kindness to one of the least of His brethren, Jesus says we do it unto Him; and so, when wives yield that subjection to their husbands that the nature of the relation implies, and do it from Christian motives, they do it as to the Lord, and He accepts it as a service done to Him.

Paul is not satisfied here, as in Col. iii. 18, 19, with a simple statement of the duties of Christian wives and husbands: he illustrates the affections proper to the relation, by comparing it with that between Christ and His Church, and so gives a very lofty ideal and a very solemn sanction to the duties he is inculcating. He seems, however, in the passage that follows, to be led by the interest of the thought to dwell on the love of Christ for His Church more fully than the mere practical purpose required; and thus there is a series of digressions, describing the spiritual relation, from which the apostle returns again and again to the earthly one.

23. **For the husband is the head of the wife, as Christ also is the head of the Church,** *being* **himself the saviour of the body.**] This verse shows how the subjection of the wife to her husband is "as to the Lord." The figure of the bridegroom applied by the prophets to Jehovah in relation to His people (Hos. i.–iii.; Isa. liv. 5; Ezek. xvi., etc.), was used by Jesus of Himself (Matt. ix. 15, xxv. 1), and Paul follows these representations in his use of it here. He had before spoken of Christ as the head, and the Church as His body, having its nourishment and direction from Him (ch. i. 22, 23, iv. 15, 16); here he applies the idea of His being the head in a somewhat different way, as head of the family or house. He is this with the fullest right; for He is Himself the saviour of the body. The idea seems to be the same as that contained in Ezekiel's parable (Ezek. xvi.), in which Israel is represented as a wretched neglected infant, exposed and ready to perish, when the Lord had pity on her, and said live, and washed and nourished and clothed, and took her for His own bride. Even so, as afterwards declared, Christ saves His Church.

24. **But as the church is subject to Christ, so let the wives also be** (*or* **are the wives also**) **to their husbands in everything.**] The spiritual pattern far transcends the earthly copy, for the husband is not, and cannot be, the saviour of the wife, as Christ is of His body, the Church. But though that cannot be, the analogy holds good in the relation of subjection in everything. This last clause is the only addition made by this verse to what was said in ver. 22, and it is probably intended to express the extent of the subjection due. It comprehends everything, *i.e.* everything belonging to family and household life. It is not needful to suppose that Paul inculcates absolute

25 husbands in every thing. Husbands, love your wives, even
as Christ also loved the church, and gave himself for it;
26 that he might sanctify and cleanse it with the washing of

slavish obedience to every command that a husband may please to lay upon a wife. That would be contrary to the spirit of his own teaching. Nor need we introduce any arbitrary limitations. What he says is, that in the conjugal relation the natural and rightful place of the husband is to be the head, and that in all domestic affairs the wife is to be subject. That he inculcates without restriction or reserve, and without prejudice to the fact that husband and wife are both alike before God, equally subject to Him and to all His ordinances, and in Christ equally partakers of that blood-bought freedom which forbids their being slaves of men. It is to be remembered that these precepts are addressed not merely to wives who had Christian husbands, but to all wives, even those whose husbands were unbelieving or pagan. It was specially important that Christian wives in such cases should act on the principles here laid down. There is no undue harshness in the view given of their duties; on the contrary, they are ennobled by the great and beautiful ideal with which they are compared; and the succeeding exhortations to husbands show that the apostle recognised their responsibilities and duties also.

25. **Husbands, love your wives, even as Christ also loved the church, and gave himself up for it:**] The duty of mutual subjection on the part of husbands takes the form of love, on account of the peculiar affectionateness of the relation. For love prompts to acts of kindness and service, and he who is doing deeds of love to another is so far subjecting himself. This is the way in which the stronger and superior can fulfil the duty of mutual subjection. "We that are strong ought to bear the infirmities of the weak, and not to please ourselves" (Rom. xv. 1). Here, too, we have the highest possible example set before us, that of Christ Himself in His love for the Church, and giving Himself up for it. The same great truth is set forth, which in the beginning of this chapter (ver. 2) had been referred to in its more general aspect and its relation to God. Here the description of Christ's work as a sacrifice is not repeated, for it is the actual blessings that our Saviour secures for us by His self-sacrificing love that are chiefly in view; because, while the exhortation there was, to have a mind or spirit like that of our Lord, here it is rather, to actual works of love. Here, too, we see that special reference of Christ's sacrifice to His own people, in virtue of which it secures for them forgiveness and sanctification, which is quite consistent with its universal relation to the whole world, as sufficient for all, suitable to all, and freely offered to all in the gospel.

26. **that he might sanctify it, having cleansed it by the washing** (*Gr.* laver) **of water with the word,**] The purpose of Christ's sacrifice is, as Paul always declares, the purification of His people; not merely their being saved from wrath, but their being delivered from sin. That deliverance is described here by two words, "sanctify" and "cleanse." Some think that these both refer to the same thing, or are done at the same time; and would translate, "that he might sanctify it, cleansing," etc., so that the last clause would describe the mode of the sanctification. But the translation in the R. V. is the more correct and natural one, and points to the cleansing as the initial act, which is followed by the work of sanctification. And there can be no doubt that by "the laver of water" is meant the sacrament of baptism. The

27 water by the word; that he might present it to himself a glorious church, not having spot, or wrinkle, or any such thing; but that it should be holy, and without blemish.

translation "washing" is barely admissible, for the word properly means the bath or basin in which the washing takes place. Paul is speaking of the Church collectively; but as that is composed of individuals, who, according to Christ's command, on being made His disciples, are to be baptized unto the name of the Father, and of the Son, and of the Holy Spirit, he ascribes here to the whole body what is true of each of its members. It is undoubtedly from sin that the Church is said to be cleansed, according to a familiar O. T. figure, and probably we need not distinguish here between cleansing from the guilt of sin by forgiveness and from the power of it by regeneration, but should include both, since the two are coincident in time, and baptism is the sign and token of both. In those days, from the nature of the case, baptism usually accompanied conversion to Christ, and was the evidence of that decisive change; and as Paul is speaking of the Church as a whole, he naturally alludes to that ordinance through which Christ brings men into its fellowship of salvation. But that he does not ascribe the cleansing of the soul from sin to the mere bath of water, appears from his adding "with (or in) the word." That means the word of God, the gospel of Jesus Christ, through faith in whom alone we are saved. "The word is added to the element, and it becomes a sacrament" (Augustine), *i.e.* a visible word, and, like the word itself, a means of grace. But our Lord's purpose of love for His people is not exhausted by this great initial act of cleansing; He gave Himself up that He might sanctify it, make it more and more thoroughly consecrated to God, and separate from the evil of the world. This is especially the work of the Holy Spirit, but is here ascribed to Christ, because, had Christ not been glorified through His sacrifice of Himself, the Spirit would not have been given, nor would He have had the perfect life and sacrifice of Christ to present to sinners as the pattern and motive of sanctification. But more particularly it is, as Paul always presents it, the work of Christ Himself; for in the work of the Spirit He is Himself active, carrying out the purpose for which He gave Himself up for the Church (comp. Gal. i. 3, 4). This is more strongly emphasised in the statement of the final end of this sanctification.

27. that he might present the church to himself a glorious *church*, not having spot or wrinkle or any such thing; but that it should be holy and without blemish.] His work for the Church is in a sense for Himself; and it is very emphatically stated here, both that He and no other is the agent, and that it is to Himself that the perfected Church is to be presented. It is then to be glorious, literally "arrayed in glory," the glory of complete moral beauty, with every spot of sin cleansed away, every wrinkle of care smoothed out, every defect removed, so that it should be holy, in soul and body fully devoted to God, and without fault of any kind. That is the ideal of Christian perfection, of which Paul had spoken in the beginning of this epistle (ch. i. 4), as the end for which God chose us in Christ before the foundation of the world. Here, doubtless, the figure of the Church as the bride, the Lamb's wife, made ready as a bride prepared for her husband, was before the apostle's mind, perhaps with a reminiscence of the description in Ps. xlv. 9—17; but to see in the preceding verse, as some do, a reference to the bride's

28 So ought men to love their wives as their own bodies: he
29 that loveth his wife loveth himself. For no man ever yet
hated his own flesh; but nourisheth and cherisheth it, even
30 as the Lord the church: for we are members of his body, of

bath before marriage is somewhat fanciful. Anyhow he returns in the next verse to the practical subject with which he is dealing.

28. So ought husbands also to love their own wives as their own bodies. He that loveth his own wife loveth himself:] The comparison indicated by the word "so" is not with what is said in the following clause, about men loving their own bodies; but, as the word "also" shows, with what was said before, about Christ's love to the Church. So, as Christ loves the Church, ought husbands also to love their own wives, in the same generous, self-denying spirit, desiring their holiness as their truest good. They ought to do this, not as if it was some extraordinary reach of goodness and benevolence, but as what is implied in the very nature of the relation, for their wives are their own, and should be as dear to them as their own bodies, *i.e.* their very selves. This is further illustrated in the following verses.

29, 30. for no man ever hated his own flesh; but nourisheth and cherisheth it, even as Christ also the church; because we are members of his body.] The statement in ver. 29 is clearly to be understood of the ordinary course of things, and abnormal cases of insanity or despair are left out of account. No man in his right mind ever hated his own flesh: such a thing is contrary to nature, and anything like it can only occur when nature is entirely disordered. As great a disorder it is, morally, when a husband does not love his wife. Thus it may be noticed, that when Christ speaks in the strongest emotional language of the duty of one who would be His disciple, "hating his own father, and mother, and wife, and children, and brethren, and sisters," He adds, "yea, and his own life also" (Luke xiv. 26). The claims of Christ are supreme, because divine; and if the nearest earthly relative would oppose them, there must be a recoil of feeling that can only be adequately expressed by "hate"; but even in that case a man's wife is no less dear than himself. The positive care described by the words "nourisheth and cherisheth" may refer to food and clothing; but they are rather general expressions for all the loving attention that the husband should show to his wife. This duty is elevated and hallowed by the comparison in the next clause to Christ's care for the Church. He has not only, as before described, given Himself for it, by a wondrous act of self-sacrifice and love; but He exerts a continual care over it, providing for all its wants, and ready to hear all its prayers. This He does, because we, who form the Church, are members of His body, *i.e.* we are as truly united to Him as the wife is to her husband, as truly His as the limbs and parts of our bodies belong to ourselves. The A. V. adds here the words "of his flesh and of his bones," which, though found in some ancient copies and quotations, are absent in the oldest and best MSS., and therefore are considered by most critics to be probably not genuine. If they are inserted, they must be understood, not as a mere expansion of "his body," but as meaning "out of, *i.e.* deriving our life from, his flesh and his bones," or His incarnate human nature. It would be an assertion that the real body of our Saviour, having flesh and bones which a spirit hath not (Luke xxiv. 39), is essential to our salvation; and would be similar to the statements in 1 John

31 his flesh, and of his bones. For this cause shall a man leave
his father and mother, and shall be joined unto his wife,
32 and they two shall be one flesh. This is a great mystery:

about the importance of confessing Jesus Christ come in flesh. But possibly
they may have been inserted, because the words in the next verse, taken from
Gen. ii. 24, seemed to require as their ground a reference to those that
precede them in Gen. ii. 23: "This is now bone of my bones, and flesh of my
flesh." Christian imagination has frequently taken the story of the formation
of Eve out of a rib in Adam's side as typical of the pierced side of the
crucified Saviour, whence flowed blood and water for the redemption and
cleansing of His Church; but there is no evidence that Paul had any such
idea in his mind here. Many first-class interpreters, of very different schools
(including Calvin), have thought that there is a reference here to the sacrament
of the Lord's Supper; but even if the doubtful clause forms part of the
text, this is far from being clear; and if that clause is not genuine, the ground
of such an allusion is removed.

31. **For this cause shall a man leave his father and mother, and shall cleave unto his wife; and the twain shall become one flesh.**] These are the words of Gen. ii. 24, and they are introduced here not properly as a quotation, as they are in 1 Cor. vi. 16 ("for, The twain, saith he, shall become one flesh"), but simply as Scripture words, used by Paul in his own name as he had done with other texts (chs. iv. 25, 26, v. 18). Also he changes slightly the opening words of the verse; for the words rendered "for this cause" are different from the literal Greek translation of the original, both in the LXX. and in Matt. xix. 5 and Mark x. 7. The preposition here used by Paul denotes opposition or correspondence, one thing being set over against or compared with another. So in Heb. xii. 3 it is said that Jesus "for the joy that was set before him endured the cross"; where "for" means "in comparison with," "in view of."[1] This meaning brings out a closer connection with what goes before than the common rendering. "Corresponding to this, viz. that we are members of Christ's body, shall a man . . . cleave unto his wife." The one union is parallel to the other, that is plainly Paul's thought here; and he uses the words of Genesis simply to describe, as they undoubtedly do, the fact of marriage. He does not say, as the ordinary translation seems to make him say, that marriage was instituted because of the union of Christ and the Church; still less does he cite the text as a typical prediction of Christ coming forth from the Father and joining Himself to the Church: he simply says, that the fact which is continually happening, of a man leaving his father and his mother and so cleaving to his wife as to become one flesh, stands over against, or is the counterpart to, Christ having made us members of His body. Christian husbands, therefore, ought to live in the marriage relation in view of this. This duty, however, is only implied; it had been stated before; and what is said here is just that as a fact this correspondence exists, and this comparison may be drawn. Such at least seems to me the best way to understand this passage, the precise connection of which is difficult.

32. **This mystery is great: but I speak in regard of Christ and of the church.**] As before explained (on ch. i. 9), "mystery" in the N. T. does

---

[1] This interpretation has not been generally adopted; but after it had occurred to me, I was glad to find that it had been also given by the Rev. Prof. G. G. Findlay in the *Expositor's Bible*: Ephesians, pp. 376, 377.

33 but I speak concerning Christ and the church. Nevertheless, let every one of you in particular so love his wife even as himself; and the wife *see* that she reverence *her* husband.
CHAP. VI. 1. Children, obey your parents in the Lord : for this

not mean a thing passing our comprehension, but simply a secret ; and here it seems to be used for the figurative significance of the words describing the marriage union which Paul had just used. This spiritual reality represented by them, though not obvious to the superficial view, is great, *i.e.* important and valuable. That is substantially what he means; and then, that there may be no mistake as to what he refers to, he adds, " but I speak in regard of Christ and of the church," *i.e.* I am using them with reference to the spiritual union of Christ and the Church, in virtue of which we are members of His body. The word by which the Latin Vulgate version renders "mystery" here and elsewhere is *sacramentum ;* and from that the Medieval and Roman Catholic theologians infer that marriage is a sacrament. But if by "sacrament" is meant anything more than a figure of spiritual things, a sense in which the fathers often used it, there is no ground for this inference; for Paul does not say, or imply, that marriage was instituted in order to be a sign and pledge of our union to Christ, but only that it may be regarded as a figure of it; and he explains that this, though of great value, is only a typical application of Scripture, or rather of the marriage union as described in Scripture.

33. **Nevertheless do ye also severally love each one his own wife even as himself; and *let* the wife *see* that she fear her husband.**] This closing verse of the paragraph is introduced by a conjunction with a slight adversative force : " nevertheless," or " however." Paul breaks off from the line of thought he has been following, and virtually says, Apart from this analogy, this " mystery " of marriage, let the plain practical duties of the conjugal relation be observed by all and each one of you. Whether or not you can understand and appreciate the comparison I have been making, you can all understand this precept, Let each one so love his own wife as himself. And then he adds the corresponding duty of the wife, that she fear her husband. The R. V. " fear " is more literal than the A. V. " reverence " ; but it conveys to our minds a stronger idea than is really contained in the original ; and "reverence" is a better translation of the sense, for undoubtedly it is that, and not fear, as we use the word, that is meant. Respect and honour for the position which the husband holds in relation to her will enable a Christian wife to fulfil the duty of submission before inculcated (ver. 22).

Paul now passes to a second relation in which the duty of mutual subjection is illustrated, that of children and parents.

VI. 1. **Children, obey your parents in the Lord: for this is right.**] The address " children " indicates their relation to their parents, and determines nothing as to their age ; but it plainly includes all, from the years when they can understand the precept, until they are of such full age as to be no longer under parental authority, though always owing filial duty. Children under age are recognised here as members of the Christian community to which the epistle is addressed, just as elsewhere Paul declares the children of believers to be holy (1 Cor. vii. 14). In their case, the mutual subjection before inculcated takes the form of obedience to their parents, and it is to be done " in the Lord," *i.e.* the Lord Jesus. These words are not meant to limit the duty to

2 is right. Honour thy father and mother, (which is the first
3 commandment with promise,) that it may be well with thee,
4 and thou mayest live long on the earth. And, ye fathers,
provoke not your children to wrath: but bring them up in the
5 nurture and admonition of the Lord. Servants, be obedient

things in accordance with the will of Christ, for they do not naturally suggest any such idea, and the necessary exception of commands that would require sin is rather to be understood as self-evident. Paul means that the obedience is to be in Christ, *i.e.* trusting in Him as the Saviour, allowing His love to surround us, and relying on His grace and strength for the ability to obey. Though the words denote the mystic union, that has been so profoundly described before, yet in these aspects it is not beyond the capacity even of young children to apprehend. As the first reason for their duty, Paul appeals to their natural sense of right; "for this is right" or just. Nature itself teaches that parents, who know so much better than their children what is good and bad, and who love and care for them with true and natural affection, should be obeyed. Then he follows up this appeal to nature by one to the word of God.

2, 3. **Honour thy father and mother (which is the first commandment with promise), that it may be well with thee, and that thou mayest live long on the earth (*or* land).**] He quotes the fifth commandment, almost exactly as it is translated by the LXX., only omitting the last words, "which the Lord thy God giveth thee," containing as they do an express reference to God's gift of Canaan to Israel, which was inapplicable under the new covenant, and to those to whom he was writing. Paul regards the moral laws given to Israel as still binding on Christians, even though some things in their original form may belong to the past economy. And he does not limit this binding authority to the precepts of the Decalogue, in which the fifth is not the first, but the only commandment with promise; but he is thinking of all the commandments that God has given, and says, that among these this is the first that has a special promise connected with it. The consideration of promises, that God has graciously given to the performance of what in itself is right, is a legitimate motive to obedience, especially for the young, whom God lovingly condescends to allure by such means. The truth of the promise is not to be judged in a mathematical or statistical way, as if obedient children must always live longer than others: it is fulfilled, if they enjoy the blessing of a happy home in which it is well with them; and if while living on the earth, one is made partaker of Christ, God fulfils His word, "with long life will I satisfy him, and will show him my salvation" (Ps. xci. 16); so that, however early he may be called hence, he may be able to say, "Lord, now lettest thou thy servant depart in peace, according to thy word, for mine eyes have seen thy salvation!"

Then follows the corresponding duty of parents.

4. **And, ye fathers, provoke not your children to wrath: but nurture them in the chastening and admonition of the Lord.**] "Fathers," in view of the quotation in ver. 2, must evidently be taken to include mothers also, and so be equivalent to "parents" (ver. 1), as the word often is. They are warned against a too harsh exercise of their authority, such as would irritate their children rather than train them aright. For the duties belonging to this relation also come under the general precept of "subjecting yourselves one to another" (ch. v. 21). It is for the parents indeed to command, and

to them that are *your* masters according to the flesh, with fear and trembling, in singleness of your heart, as unto Christ ;

for the children to obey ; but the parents' office of commanding is to be exercised for the good of the children, and so they are to be subservient to their children's welfare. "The children," says Paul (2 Cor. xii. 14), "ought not to lay up for the parents, but the parents for the children." Thus they are enjoined, not only to be gentle and loving in their rule, so as not to provoke them to anger, but to give themselves faithfully to their upbringing. In the positive part of this precept, the revisers have made the expressions correspond more exactly with the original. For "bring up" they have substituted "nurture"; because it is the same word that is rendered "nourisheth" in ch. v. 29, and conveys the idea of supplying what is needful for life and growth. Then the noun rendered "nurture" in A. V. is very common in N. T., and is almost always rendered "chastening" or "chastisement" in English. It includes, however, more than that, and denotes discipline, or education in general, literally the training of children; and we can hardly doubt that Paul meant it here in that wider sense. "Admonition" means, literally, laying before the mind, and indicates that while children must in the first place be trained to obedience to what they cannot be told the reason of, yet, as their understanding advances, appeal should be made to it, so that their obedience may as early as possible become an intelligent and loving one. This is a means of guarding against the danger of irritation, which is apt to arise, when authority is needlessly arbitrary, or is made to appear so. This education and admonition is to be "of the Lord," here again the Lord Jesus. That is, it is to be such, that in it the Lord Himself is training and teaching the children by means of the parents. They are to seek to know what His mind and will is for their children, to teach them as they have themselves been taught by the Lord, and to lead and encourage them to seek the Lord Jesus Himself to be the guide of their youth.

The third relation, to which Paul applies the principle of mutual subjection (ch. v. 21), is that of servants and masters. Since, in fact, the servants were then generally slaves, it has been thought by some that by bidding them be obedient to their masters, the apostles gave sanction to the institution of slavery, as it then existed ; and this has been applied in two opposite ways, either to defend slavery or to discredit the morality of the N. T. But in truth neither inference is fair. The remarkable thing here is, not that slaves should be exhorted to obedience, but that they should be addressed as Christian brethren at all. Their admission, on terms of perfect equality, to the community of believers, established the principle which inevitably led to their emancipation, wherever the spirit of Christianity has prevailed ; and we need only compare the way in which the N. T. speaks of them with the tone of contemporary heathen writers, to see the difference of spirit in this respect. It would have been wrong for the apostles to have directly denounced slavery, for that would have tended to provoke a servile revolt, which could only have produced crime and misery, and led to no good. They were more wisely guided, to bring even to slaves the salvation of Christ, and show them that even in their servitude they could have true blessedness and freedom to obey the laws of Christ, giving them at once religious equality, and ultimately securing their social equality also.

5. Servants (*Gr.* bond-servants), be obedient unto them that according to the flesh are your masters (*Gr.* lords), with fear and trembling, in single-

6 not with eye-service, as men-pleasers; but as the servants of
7 Christ, doing the will of God from the heart; with good will
8 doing service, as to the Lord, and not to men: knowing that
whatsoever good thing any man doeth, the same shall he
9 receive of the Lord, whether *he be* bond or free. And, ye

ness of your heart as unto Christ;] The clause "according to the flesh" is inserted to remind them that the relation in which they are under the control of fellow-men is only an external one; their masters have by human laws a right to command their bodies and service; but they are not lords of their souls or consciences. Paul also uses the gentler of two words by which masters might be designated, one that might also be applied to a ruler over free men, or even as a mere title of courtesy. Yet though the relation is but an external one, he would not have slaves perform their duties in a merely outward and mechanical way, but with due respect for their earthly masters, and feeling of the power they had over them, and also with no duplicity of mind, but with the single desire of doing their duty, knowing that it is Christ's will that they should serve faithfully, and that in so obeying their masters they are obeying their Saviour.

6. **not in the way of eye-service, as men-pleasers; but as servants** (*Gr.* bond-servants) **of Christ, doing the will of God from the heart** (*Gr.* soul);] This illustrates more particularly the foregoing precept. Eye-service is a graphic expression for obedience that is rendered only when the master's eye is thought to be upon them; and such is the service that will be rendered by those who look no higher than the earthly master, and desire only to please him. They will not be careful to do work that he will never see, and the absence of which he will never blame. But those who are servants of Christ will know that their obedience is part of their duty to Him, and of the will of God for them. Thus in view of Him who searches the heart and sees in secret, they will take care that their work is honest and thorough. The words "from the heart" may be connected with the following verse, and some prefer to take them so; but they belong more naturally to this one. In any case, they mean that the mind is to be in the work, so that whatever they are required to do they endeavour to do it well.

7. **with good will doing service, as unto the Lord, and not unto men:**] This refers to the feelings they should have to their masters, as the former clause did to those with which they should regard their work. Paul uses no exaggerated phrase here; he does not speak of love, or admiration, or reverence; such feelings might sometimes be impossible: but he desires that in their work they should be well disposed to their master, having his interests really at heart, and desiring to do him good. This they can do, if they are doing service as to the Lord, for they know that His law is summed up in love one to another.

8. **knowing that whatsoever good thing each one doeth, the same shall he receive again from the Lord, whether** *he be* **bond or free.**] This is an encouragement to the duties that have been enjoined. Such service as has been described may often be thankless and unappreciated by earthly masters. They may never know how conscientiously and faithfully their slaves have been doing their work, when their eye was not upon them; they may take their service as a matter of course, and give no word of praise or acknowledgment; they may unjustly blame, and a slave may be punished,

masters, do the same things unto them, forbearing threatening:
knowing that your Master also is in heaven; neither is there

as Joseph was, for his very faithfulness to duty. But though human masters may be ignorant or contemptuous or unjust, no truly good work shall in the end go without acknowledgment and reward. This shall be given by the Lord, literally "the Master," for it is significant that in this passage masters of bond-servants are described by the same name as that habitually given to Christ (*Kyrios*). Conversely, the name which more strictly denotes the relation of a master to a slave (*despotes*), and is so used in 1 Tim. vi. 1, 2; Tit. ii. 9; 1 Pet. ii. 18, is applied to Christ and to God in Luke ii. 29; Acts iv. 24; 2 Pet. ii. 1; Jude 4; Rev. vi. 10. In most of these passages the context indicates a reason for the use of the special name; here manifestly the word is chosen in order to elevate and ennoble the position of slaves.

The statement here, of the bestowal of righteous rewards by Christ upon all who have done any good work, is in harmony with what Paul frequently teaches, without suspecting it to be at all inconsistent with his gospel of salvation by grace, through faith, without works of law. This passage is noticeable, because it is the only reference in this epistle to Christ's coming again as Judge of all, a doctrine which is very prominent in Paul's earlier epistles, and was firmly held by him to the last.

Then follows, as in the other relations, a corresponding exhortation to masters about their duty to their slaves.

9. **And, ye masters (*Gr.* lords), do the same things unto them, and forbear threatening: knowing that both their Master and yours is in heaven, and there is no respect of persons with him.]** This is the most striking and even startling application of the general principle of ch. v. 21, "subjecting yourselves one to another in the fear of Christ," that Paul should bid masters, not only, as in Col. iv. 1, "render to their servants that which is just and equal," but do the same things to them. The reciprocity of duties in the cases of husbands and wives, and of parents and children, is more obvious, and did not need to be emphasised; but it is strongly asserted here, in the extreme case of masters and slaves. Doing "the same things" cannot be understood with literal exactness, for it cannot be the duty of the master to obey his own servants. But it may be taken to indicate that, as the servant benefits his master by his work, so the master should benefit his servants by his care and supervision. Even if they be slaves, a Christian master will always feel that he has a duty to his servants, as well as they to him; and in regard to the good-will, which is the most essential thing that has been enjoined on servants, the precept to masters to do the same applies in the fullest and strictest sense. They are further enjoined to forbear threatening, literally "the threatening," namely, that which is so common as a means by which masters try to secure the obedience of their servants. This is to be let alone, their rule is not to be one of terror, but of duty enforced in a reasonable and kindly way. It is worthy of notice that in enforcing the duties of masters to their servants, Paul does not condescend to appeal to motives of mere pity or compassion, that might move them to mitigate the hard lot of their slaves, but to considerations of justice and equity, thus recognising even the slave as a man and a brother. The principles of these exhortations are applicable to the modern relations of capitalists and labourers, employers and employed; and have much need to be applied to them. They indicate, what is borne out by the most advanced results of political economy, that

10 respect of persons with him. Finally, my brethren, be strong
11 in the Lord, and in the power of his might. Put on the
whole armour of God, that ye may be able to stand against

there is a mutual benefit in such relations; and that, if labour does much for capital, it is no less true that capital does a great deal for labour. Each benefits the other, and the relations between them should be regulated by the golden rule of mutual good-will.

The motive by which Paul ultimately enforces his injunctions to masters is, like that of those to servants, the knowledge that there is in heaven one who is Master of both alike, and that with Him there is no respect of persons; that is, that He does not favour or accept anyone on account of any outward appearance, or extrinsic position or relation, but looks to the man himself, in his own essential character. Rank, riches, nationality, learning, reputation,—all these are things that belong to a man, but they are not the man himself; they are as it were garments, but not the very being of the man. What God looks to is, not what a man has about him, or what part he plays in the drama of life, but what he has in him, and the one thing needful is that newness of life which comes through faith in Jesus Christ. This is a familiar Pauline thought, appropriately and emphatically recalled by these closing words.

VI. 10-20. *Call to arms against spiritual foes.*—The apostle now closes with a call to his readers to be strong against their formidable spiritual enemies, and a description of the means of defence which they may and should use against them.

10. **Finally (*or* from henceforth), be strong (*Gr.* be made powerful) in the Lord, and in the strength of his might.**] The marginal reading "from henceforth," which would make the words refer to the remaining time of their life, though quite grammatical, the same words being so rendered in Gal. vi. 17, is not so natural here. They simply mean, "for the rest," viz. of what I have to say to you: all that I have now to add is this one exhortation. The passive form, "be made powerful," shows that the strength we need lies not in ourselves, but is to be received from without, from the Lord. It is in Him we are to be powerful, or able for the work we have to do; and, as the apostle says elsewhere, it is when we really are and feel ourselves weak, that the strength of Christ is made perfect in us. It is our part to abide in Him by a genuine faith working by love, and then we shall be enabled, by His strength supporting and invigorating us, to perform the duties and endure the trials to which He may call us. Thus this is an exhortation not only to courage, but also to humility and self-distrust; for nothing can so fatally weaken us as vain confidence in our own strength. For the distinction between strength and might, see above on ch. i. 19.

11. **Put on the whole armour of God, that ye may be able to stand against the wiles of the devil.**] Here Paul proceeds to remind us that, while the primary requisite for strength is to abide in Christ, there are certain means that we must employ for our defence; and these he calls the whole armour, or panoply, of God, the various parts of which he describes in the following verses. This metaphor was probably suggested to him by the scenes and sights that met his view in his military confinement at Rome; but evidently he had long turned it over in his own mind, for, as we shall see, he connects almost every piece of the armour with some O. T. passage; and the

12 the wiles of the devil. For we wrestle not against flesh and blood, but against principalities, against powers, against the rulers of the darkness of this world, against spiritual

germ of the idea is found in his very earliest epistle, 1 Thess. v. 8. The purpose of the panoply is that we may be able to stand against the wiles of the devil. Had we merely work to do, armour would not be needed; but since we have also a warfare to wage, we must be armed. Our great enemy is the being who has been mentioned before in the epistle as the prince of the power of the air (ch. ii. 2), and is here called by his more common name, "the devil," *i.e.* the adversary or accuser. He is viewed here, however, as having for his aim to lead us into sin, and using for that purpose wiles, stratagems devised by great and unscrupulous wisdom. Whatever may be the mysteries connected with the existence of such a being, it is not wise for practical purposes to ignore the warnings given us in the Bible. It may be that we cannot distinguish Satanic temptation from the allurements of the world, and the evil remaining in our own hearts; but it is well to remember that the evil against which we have to contend assails us in a more subtle and deceptive way than what we know as human solicitations. There is a moral atmosphere, a time-spirit, deceptive views, and plausible sophisms, that operate on the soul as opiates or intoxicants; and, considering the undoubted reality of such influences, we may well say that the existence of Satan is at least a judgment of value (*Werthurtheil*); we ought to act as if we had such a great spiritual enemy.

12. For our wrestling is not against flesh and blood, but against the principalities, against the powers, against the world-rulers of this darkness, against the spiritual *hosts* of wickedness in the heavenly *places*.] This description of the enemies against which we have to contend, is made much more exact in the R. V., which introduces the definite articles, that point back to the superhuman powers mentioned before, as put under the feet of Christ (ch. i. 21), and as learning, through the Church, the manifold wisdom of God (ch. iii. 10). They are here contrasted with flesh and blood, *i.e.* merely human powers; and they are described (1) in reference to their rank in the scale of being; they are such as bear rule and authority, not indeed so as to have a right to command us, but so as to be formidable by their order and organisation. (2) In reference to the sway they actually exercise, they are called "world-rulers of this darkness," dominating the ungodly world as long as it is in its present state of ignorance of God and Christ. And (3) in reference to the subtlety of their assaults, they are "spiritual hosts of wickedness." By this is meant not merely immaterial beings, but such enthusiastic impulses or utterances as seemed to be truly prophetic, though really tending to lead astray; such as John refers to when he bids his readers believe not every spirit, but try the spirits whether they are of God (1 John iv. 1). Perhaps Paul would say that he had to contend with such spiritualities of evil, when, on his last journey to Jerusalem, the prophecies that foretold in every city that bonds and imprisonment awaited him, tended to turn him from his purpose.

As in his former references to superhuman beings, Paul does not here intend to give us information about their nature and mode of activity, but to bring out practical truths bearing on our life and conduct; and here he would have us remember that the evil by which we are tempted is not a mere

13 wickedness in high *places*. Wherefore take unto you the whole armour of God, that ye may be able to withstand in 14 the evil day, and having done all, to stand. Stand therefore,

isolated thing, but a consistent system to which, if we yield in any one point, we shall be in danger of being entirely enslaved; that it is the influence that rules and guides the world; and that it may often approach us in the guise of a messenger of God, an angel of light.

The last clause, "in the heavenlies," is taken by many of the best interpreters in connection with the third of these designations, as denoting the abode of these spiritualities of evil; and so it would be parallel to "the air" in ch. ii. 2, and express the popular idea as to the seat of evil spirits. But "in the heavenlies" is the same phrase that has occurred four times before in this epistle, and in all the previous places it has an ideal sense, denoting the place, or state, of nearness to God and elevation over the world, to which Christ Himself, and all who believe in Him, have been raised. So far from being identified with the air, it seems rather to be distinguished from it (see on chs. i. 20, ii. 2, 6); and it is arbitrary and unnatural to change its meaning here, as the A. V. has done by rendering it "high places." It seems preferable to connect it with "our wrestling," so that it may indicate that while we are, as before described, in the heavenlies, in a higher and more blessed position than even these superhuman powers, they may attack us there, and seek to throw us down. We must not suppose that because we have been quickened with Christ, and raised up with Him, and made to sit with Him in the heavenlies, we are safe from all enemies. Though we are converted, and forgiven and accepted by God, and renewed, we are not free from temptation and conflict with evil. But we are to keep our position; not to descend to lower ground; but, as God's beloved children in Christ, we are to resist, in the heavenlies, the assaults that may be made upon us.

13. **Wherefore take up the whole armour of God, that ye may be able to withstand in the evil day, and, having done all, to stand.**] The need of the divine panoply is very pointedly deduced from the nature of the foes we have to meet; and hence it may be inferred that by the armour that is to protect us from them, are meant fixed and settled habits of the graces or virtues afterwards enumerated. If we had only to contend against direct persuasions or temptations to evil from our fellow-men, we might be able to resist them simply by deliberate acts of refusal, or resolutions of firmness and fidelity. But since our purposes are liable to be sapped, and our convictions to be undermined, by subtle unseen influences, from example, and spiritual environment, we cannot safely trust to being able to meet every solicitation to evil at the moment it arises; for it may steal on us insensibly before we are aware of its nature. To be safe from such attractions, we need to be fortified by habits of goodness that will counteract the influence of the moral climate in which we live; and if they do not repel its allurements, will at least give us time to summon up our strength and resolution for a determined defence. Peter, though honestly resolved to follow Jesus even to prison and to death, found his resolution fail him in the hour of darkness, because he had not fortified it by watching and prayer. Thus this exhortation, though highly imaginative in its form, is most practical in its meaning, and shows a deep and true insight into human nature. It adds an important lesson to what has been said before as to the graces and duties of Christians,

having your loins girt about with truth, and having on the
15 breastplate of righteousness; and your feet shod with the

by enforcing the necessity of these being acquired as habits, and the protection that is thus afforded.

The Christian's panoply is said to be "of God," as provided and bestowed by Him; and also because, as we shall see, some at least of its pieces are described in O. T. passages, which Paul has in his mind, as worn by God or by the Messiah. Since the apostle has called on us already to put on the new man, which after God hath been created in righteousness and holiness of truth (ch. iv. 24), and to be imitators of God (ch. v. 1), we need not scruple to find here the idea that we are to put on, as our armour, the moral attributes with which God Himself is clothed. But though this armour is God's, and given us by Him, we are called to be active on our part in taking it up and putting it on, just as we are exhorted to work out our own salvation with fear and trembling, because it is God that worketh in us both to will and to do. From the nature of the case, habits cannot be acquired without our own action, though without the aid of God's Spirit we cannot act aright.

The object is, first, "that ye may be able to withstand in the evil day." This note of time probably refers not to any definite period, but to whatever might be a time of assault and temptation to any one, when he would need strength to stand against the attacks of evil. Then the final goal is indicated, "having done all," accomplished your whole warfare and withstood all your foes, to stand. This may indicate, that even in the hour of victory there is danger of falling through self-confidence; and that the warning must ever be kept in mind, "Let him that thinketh he standeth take heed lest he fall."

14. **Stand therefore, having girded your loins with truth, and having put on the breastplate of righteousness,**] The first piece of the panoply that he mentions, is the girdle about the loins, which serves to brace the frame for free and vigorous action; and the grace corresponding to this is truth. This suggests the words in Isa. xi. 5, where of the Saviour promised to spring out of the root of Jesse it is said, "righteousness shall be the girdle of his loins, and faithfulness (the same word as "truth" here) the girdle of his reins." From this it appears that it is not the thing that is true that is meant, though the word is often used in that sense, but truthfulness in the soul, sincerity, the being of the truth, loving and doing truth. This has been inculcated before in this epistle (ch. iv. 15–25) as a means of Christian growth and perfection; here the habit of it is set before us as a means of defence. It is really analogous to the girdle, for a sincere love of truth makes a man free and unembarrassed to move wherever truth may call; whereas those who are not sincere and upright even with themselves, are ever apt to be entangled and hampered in their movements.

Next comes the breastplate, and that is righteousness. This, too, recalls a passage in Isaiah (lix. 17), where it is said of God, "he put on righteousness as a breastplate." And in 1 Thess. v. 8, Paul counsels "putting on the breastplate of faith and love." Hence it appears that this, too, denotes a quality in us, not the imputed righteousness of Christ, which the word sometimes means, but that personal righteousness in which we are renewed after the image of God, and which consists of loyalty and love to God and man. This is appropriately compared to the breastplate, whose function it is to protect the vital organs, the heart and lungs. For without that righteousness

16 preparation of the gospel of peace; above all, taking the shield of faith, wherewith ye shall be able to quench all the

which is required by the law of love, the believer's spiritual life would be exposed to injury in its very seat and centre.

15. **and having shod your feet with the preparation of the gospel of peace;**] Strong shoes or boots formed an important part of the Roman soldier's equipment, insomuch that the military boot was sometimes used as a description of the service. What Paul compares to it in the Christian's armour is the readiness or alacrity for service which the glad tidings of peace give; for that seems to be the best explanation of the connection, the preparation produced by the gospel. By peace we shall then understand peace with God, reconciliation through Christ, which is the great theme and promise of the gospel. When a man has had his lips touched with fire from the altar, and heard the gracious words, "Lo, this hath touched thy lips; and thine iniquity is taken away, and thy sin purged," then he is ready, on hearing the voice of the Lord, saying, "Whom shall I send, and who will go for us?" to reply promptly, "Here am I, Lord; send me." Without this gospel, the very truth with which he confesses his sin, and the righteousness that makes him feel its evil, would only plunge him in despair.

16. **withal taking up the shield of faith, wherewith ye shall be able to quench all the fiery darts of the evil** *one*.] The revisers have altered the A. V. "above all," because the preponderance of testimony of MSS. and versions is in favour of "in all"; but in any case the meaning would seem to be, not that this is the most important piece of the armour, but that we are to be sure to take it in addition to or along with all the rest. The reason is, because the enemy not only uses weapons that cut or thrust, but shoots arrows wrapped round with lighted tow, which burn as they strike, and may of a sudden involve the warrior in flame. Against ordinary spears or swords or arrows, it might be sufficient to have the vital parts well protected; and a wound on an exposed limb might be of little danger. But when fiery darts are flying about, in order to be safe, one must have means of keeping them away from his person, and, if possible, extinguishing the flame; and this can be done by the shield, since those used by the Roman soldiers were large and oblong, such as could cover most of the body, and might be moved in various directions to meet any coming dart and dash it to the ground. In speaking of fiery darts, Paul may have simply intended to bring out the terrible nature of the assaults of the evil one; but it is possible that he may also have wished to indicate, that suggestions of evil are like fire-fraught arrows in this, that they have the power of kindling a flame of passion in us which may rage through our whole nature. Such, certainly, is the deadly effect of many a seemingly trifling impression, a word, or a sight, or a thought. Against this danger our safeguard is the shield of faith. With his mind running so much on the expressions of O. T., the apostle could not have been unmindful of the many passages that speak of God Himself, or His faithfulness, as being a shield to His people (Gen. xv. 1; 2 Sam. xxii. 3; Ps. lix. 11, lxxxiv. 9, xci. 4, cxliv. 2); nor does he say anything contrary to them. For faith is that by which we lay hold of God as our Saviour; it derives all its power from its object, and it can be called a shield to us, just because it unites us with God our shield, and makes us safe under His faithfulness and truth. The kindling and inflaming power of suggestions from without, whether to repining against God, or to anger, or evil desire, or despair, is best met by

17 fiery darts of the wicked. And take the helmet of salvation, and the sword of the Spirit, which is the word of God:

trust in God, which will make us feel that He is our portion, and that we must not be disquieted or perturbed in mind.

17. **And take the helmet of salvation,**] This is parallel to what Paul had written in 1 Thess. v. 8, "for a helmet the hope of salvation"; and on both occasions probably he had in his mind Isa. lix. 17, where it is said of God, "he put on . . . a helmet of salvation upon his head." With these passages may be compared also, Ps. cxl. 7: "O God the Lord, the strength of my salvation, thou hast covered my head in the day of battle." The purely defensive armour, that has been described before, might suffice for one who was only to be kept safe, and who might lurk inactive behind a broad shield. But for one who is to take a bold and active part in the warfare, and lift up his head above his breastplate and shield, a helmet is needful; else as soon as he attempted to stir, he might receive a deadly wound. Now, as the Christian soldier is called to be active in his Captain's service, he needs something corresponding to the head-piece that enables the helmeted warrior to move forward fearlessly into the midst of the fray. Such a helmet is the sure hope or experience of salvation. This is not, indeed, absolutely essential to Christian life; but it is a great help to Christian work and activity. One who is ever in doubt of his state before God, and has no well-founded hope that he shall be saved at last, may be a true child of God; but his spiritual life is weak and imperfect; he has need to grow up to fuller maturity and strength. Assurance of salvation is a thing that may be attained by believers, and that ought to be sought after. Paul has indicated in this epistle how the Holy Spirit of God is the seal and earnest of our inheritance; and all the N. T. writers teach in various ways the importance and the way of gaining true assurance (see Heb. vi.; 2 Pet. i. 1-11; 1 John v.).

But the figure of the helmet shows that this hope is to be sought as a help to work for Christ, not as a mere comfort or joy to ourselves; it is not a pillow on which to recline the head in indolent comfort, but a helmet to enable us to lift it up in active service of our Lord in face of difficulty and danger. If it is sought for this purpose, God will not refuse to grant it; but if any desire it merely for their own comfort, and if they had it, would sit down contented, as if they need do nothing more, in very mercy the Captain of our salvation will withhold it from such, to whom it would be not a help to victory, but an allurement to ruin. This piece of armour fitly prepares for the one weapon of attack mentioned along with the defensive panoply.

and the sword of the Spirit, which is the word of God:] The relative "which" here, by its neuter gender, points more properly to "the Spirit" than to "the sword," though the form may be explained by the gender of the noun here rendered "word." But in truth all the three ideas are identified. As salvation is not different from the helmet, but symbolised by it, so the sword is not something distinct from the Spirit, but is simply its figurative name; and the Spirit as the sword of the Christian soldier is explained to be the word of God. The term so rendered here is not the most common and comprehensive one for God's revelation of His will, but one that emphasises the notion of oral utterance; and it suggests that what is meant is not the word of God as it comes to the believer, for that has already been mentioned in this panoply, under the name of the gospel of peace, with the preparation of which our feet are shod; but rather the word as spoken by the believer,

18 praying always with all prayer and supplication in the Spirit,
and watching thereunto with all perseverance and supplication
19 for all saints; and for me, that utterance may be given unto

and wielded by him as a weapon to destroy falsehood and evil, and to defend and promote the right. In the vision of the glorified Saviour to John (Rev. i. 16), it is said that "out of his mouth proceeded a sharp two-edged sword"; and in Heb. iv. 12 the word of God is declared to be living and powerful, sharper than any two-edged sword. It may and should be so as spoken by Christ's servants, for, says Peter, "if any man speak, let him speak as oracles of God" (1 Pet. iv. 11). But it is the Spirit of God dwelling in the soul that alone can enable a man thus to speak. It was by the Holy Spirit that the men of God were moved through whom the word came; prophecy was the effect and sign of the presence of the Spirit; and if we would wield the word of God effectively as a sword, we must not merely repeat its sentences by rote, but be filled with the Spirit, of which it is the utterance, and thus apply it in the ways and for the purposes for which it was designed by God. Thus we can understand the close association and identification of word and Spirit here.

Along with the use of this divine panoply, each part of which is so well fitted to serve its purpose, the apostle urges the necessity of continual prayer.

18. **with all prayer and supplication praying at all seasons in the Spirit, and watching thereunto in all perseverance and supplication for all the saints,**] The R. V., by a change in the order of the words, has more exactly represented the original, and shown its connection with what goes before. All the Christian habits that are represented by the several pieces of armour, are to be attained by prayer, as well as by the use of suitable means; and this is especially true of that mentioned last, the sword of the Spirit. The injunction to prayer is, therefore, appropriate, and it is very emphatic. There is to be all prayer, *i.e.* all the elements of which prayer is made up, *e.g.* adoration, confession, petition, thanksgiving. And while "prayer" is a general term, including every devotional approach to God, there is associated with it "supplication," which expresses especially the sense of need and urgent desire for its relief. Then it is to be at all seasons, whether of prosperity or adversity; for in every one we have need of the help and blessing of God. It is to be in the Spirit; for, as we have the promise of the Spirit when we speak for God, so we have also when we speak to Him: He helps our infirmities, making intercession for us, and enabling us to cry, Abba, Father. Once more, our prayer is not to be narrow and self-centred, but as wide as the Church and cause of God, "for all the saints." Even in view of our own personal growth and perfecting in holiness, a wide and catholic interest in the whole people of God is of importance in our prayers; and this should not be absent in personal devotion, still less in common prayer. Paul also tells us we ought to make an earnest business of our prayers, "watching thereto," *i.e.* keeping ourselves on the alert, lest, like the disciples in Gethsemane, we be overcome with sleep or drowsiness when we have special call or precious opportunities for prayer.

From this Paul passes, by a natural and pathetic transition, to a request that he may be himself remembered in their prayers.

19. **and on my behalf, that utterance may be given unto me in**

me, that I may open my mouth boldly, to make known the
20 mystery of the gospel, for which I am an ambassador in
bonds ; that therein I may speak boldly, as I ought to speak.

opening my mouth, to make known with boldness the mystery of the gospel,] He would not have them think of him as one so far raised above common infirmities as to have no need of their prayers, even in reference to his apostolic work ; for he begs them to pray on his behalf not that he might be released from his confinement, though for that, too, he welcomes the intercessions of his friends at Colossæ (Philem. 22), but that he may be enabled to speak with freedom and boldness for Christ. The phrase "opening the mouth" is used in Scripture for the beginning of an important declaration, especially on a solemn occasion, as in our Lord's Sermon on the Mount (Matt. v. 2). Paul is anxious that, when he has the opportunity of setting forth the gospel, he should be enabled to speak with freedom and boldness. We know from his writings how much of these qualities appeared in his utterance, and with what decision and vigour he could speak in defence and exposition of the Christian message ; but here we learn that for that frank and unfearing speech he relied, not merely on his natural intrepidity of character, but on the help of God received in answer to prayer.

20. for which I am an ambassador in chains (*Gr*. a chain); that in it I may speak boldly, as I ought to speak.] He recurs here to the thought of his imprisonment, of which he had spoken before in a different connection. The word rendered "am an ambassador" is more exactly "act as an ambassador," or "perform an embassy"; it is not so much his office as his work that he has in mind, and the expression is a paradoxical one, for the persons of ambassadors were by the law of nations inviolable, so that "an ambassador in chains" might seem a contradiction in terms. But the idea is not that he is one whose privilege has been violated, but that his embassy is one which can and must be carried on, even though the bearer of it be wrongfully kept a prisoner. The literal rendering, "a chain," may be meant to refer to the actual manner of his confinement, since he was fastened by the wrist with a single chain to a Roman soldier. So in 2 Tim. i. 16 he speaks of "my chain." But the singular is sometimes used for bonds in general, so that this allusion cannot be pressed. Anyhow, his great concern is that, chained as he is, he may be able to perform properly his gospel embassy. "In it" is in the gospel, the message of God's good-will, even to those by whom he was imprisoned and persecuted. He desires to speak boldly, literally "saying all," keeping back nothing through favour or fear of man, but declaring fully the whole counsel of God. This is how he had preached the gospel at Ephesus (see Acts xx. 20–27), and this is how he prays, and desires their prayers, that he may be enabled to speak it in Rome also, even though constantly shackled to heathen soldiers. What a light do these simple words throw on the courage, the faithfulness, and the modesty of the great apostle ! He utters no complaint ; he regards his testimony for Jesus amid all his difficulties as simply what he ought to do ; and for this he desires help through the prayers of the believers in Asia.

VI. 21-24. *Conclusion.*—Paul desires also that his readers should know how things are with him ; but instead of writing about these matters himself, as he does with such pathetic frankness in his letter to the Philippians, he refers them to the friend who was to be the bearer of this epistle and also

21 But that ye also may know my affairs, *and* how I do, Tychicus, a beloved brother and faithful minister in the Lord, shall
22 make known to you all things : whom I have sent unto you for the same purpose, that ye might know our affairs, and

of that to the Colossians, and he does so almost in the same words as in that epistle (Col. iv. 7, 8).

21. But that ye also may know my affairs, how I do, Tychicus, the beloved brother and faithful minister in the Lord, shall make known to you all things:] The word "also" here, which does not occur in Col. iv. 7, seems to refer to the Christians at Colossæ, and to show that this epistle was written after the one to them : "that ye as well as they, to whom I have already written, may know my affairs." "How I do" has the same idiomatic meaning in Greek as in English, how I fare ; referring not specially to his action, but rather to his condition. Tychicus is known to us from Acts xx. 4 as an Asian Christian, who was among those who accompanied Paul on his last journey to Jerusalem, taking charge of the collections from the Gentile churches for the poor saints at Jerusalem, and themselves appearing as the first-fruits of the Greek world to Christ. For this honourable mission he must have been commended as a man of high character and tried faithfulness. He was now with Paul at Rome, though when and how he had gone there we do not know. He had been again with Paul when he wrote from his Roman prison his latest letter, the second to Timothy, in which he says that he has sent Tychicus to Ephesus. He was thus one of a number of the apostle's friends and disciples, who did good service in acting as messengers and delegates to distant churches ; and he is here described as a beloved brother and faithful minister in the Lord. The latter phrase does not necessarily imply that he had been set apart to office in the Church, though it does not exclude that ; but it may refer more probably to such services as he had rendered and was rendering to the cause of Christ by his journeys. In mentioning him as one who would satisfy their desire to know about their beloved teacher, it is not official position in the Church, but personal friendship and faithfulness to him, that he naturally speaks of.

22. whom I have sent unto you for this very purpose, that ye may know our state, and that he may comfort your hearts.] The visit of Tychicus to them was not a mere accidental thing, of which Paul availed himself to give them information about his state, but a journey that the apostle had himself arranged for that very purpose. The mention of this adds to the grace and friendliness of this reference to him, and makes the conclusion of this epistle, though very bare and destitute of personal messages, not at all cold or hard, but expressive of a high degree of mutual interest and affection between Paul and those to whom he writes. He has sent a much-loved friend, with an express commission to tell the disciples in Asia all that is happening to him in Rome. He is also confident that what Tychicus has to tell will tend to their comfort and encouragement. This shows that on the whole things were well with him, and favourable to the progress of the gospel. How this was so, he has explained at length in his letter to the Philippians, written not very long either before or after this one. Also in the letter to Philemon, sent along with this, he bids him prepare a lodging for him ; for he trusts that through the prayers of his friends he will shortly be released, and enabled to visit them. His appeal to Cæsar had not yet been disposed of,

23 *that* he might comfort your hearts. Peace *be* to the brethren,
and love with faith, from God the Father, and the Lord Jesus
24 Christ. Grace *be* with all them that love our Lord Jesus
Christ in sincerity. Amen.

such had been the law's delay; but the cause was now soon to be decided. And
as the mere profession of Christianity had not yet come to be regarded as a
crime, and both Felix and Festus had considered the special accusations of the
Jews to involve no criminal offence, it was likely that sentence would be given
in his favour. So Paul evidently expected, though he knew that before such
a judge as Nero, or any of his officials, an opposite result was possible; and
he was prepared for either issue. Whether this actually took place, we have
no direct and certain information; but it is most likely that Paul was acquitted
and released—(1) from the reasons that led him to expect it; (2) from the
Epistles to Timothy and Titus, which cannot easily be explained except as
referring to journeys of Paul later than this, and to a subsequent imprisonment
at Rome; and (3) from reports current in the succeeding ages that Paul was
thus released, and pursued further labours. But however that may have
been, the hearts of the Asian Christians would be cheered by the account of how
Paul was of good courage, and how the gospel was making progress in the
capital.

There are no personal messages or greetings in this epistle, either from any
of Paul's companions, or from him to any individuals among those to whom
it is addressed. This is best accounted for on the view for which the more
direct grounds have been given in the Introduction, that it was addressed not
to the Ephesian Christians alone, but to those in other places of the province
of Asia to whom Tychicus would have instructions to carry it. But it closes
with a twofold blessing, to those to whom it was addressed, and to all
Christians.

23. **Peace be to the brethren, and love with faith, from God the Father
and the Lord Jesus Christ.**] "The brethren" would seem to mean the
whole body of those to whom the epistle was sent, all the members of the
various churches into which they were formed, perhaps mentioned in this way
rather than directly in the second person, because it would not come to them
all together, and he would have each of their assemblies know that the
blessing was intended for all alike. There seems no reason to suppose that
the special blessing of peace is mentioned here because any tendency to
divisions made it seem particularly suitable: it is the great religious privilege
of peace with God, bringing with it peace of conscience and heart, for which
the apostle prays on their behalf. To that he adds "love with faith," a somewhat
unusual form, though the connection of the two graces is familiar to him.
Faith works by love; and he prays that they may have, from God the Father
and the Lord Jesus Christ, that love which is the fruit and evidence of faith.

24. **Grace be with all them that love our Lord Jesus Christ in uncorruptness.**] Grace is the parting wish with which, in some form or other,
Paul closes all his epistles; and it is not used by James, Peter, Jude, or John
in his letters, though it is found in the close of the Apocalypse and of the
Epistle to the Hebrews. These differences in manner contribute to show the
distinct individuality of the N. T. writers. But while, in closing all his other
letters, Paul prays for grace, the grace of our Lord Jesus Christ, for those
whom he addresses, in this one alone the prayer for grace has a wider scope,

and adds to a blessing sought for the original readers, one invoked on all who love our Lord Jesus Christ. The reason of this probably is, that this epistle has been so much occupied with that one great body in which Christ has reconciled Jews and Gentiles alike to God and to one another. The thought of this has been in the apostle's mind from the beginning to the end of the epistle; the sense that this great unity is not a mere ideal or theory, but has been showing itself to be a reality, was probably what moved him to the rapturous outburst of praise with which the epistle opens, apparently so abruptly; and the desire to exhibit this to the readers has been one great motive to the line of the teaching contained in it. Hence, while on other occasions he might feel it enough to pray for grace to those whom he was writing, he cannot close this epistle without invoking this blessing on that great body of which he has been thinking. He describes it in such a way as to bring out that the real ground of its greatness, and its charm for him, is its relation to Christ, and that it is not merely the body as a whole, but the men and women who compose it, that are dear to him. All them that love our Lord Jesus Christ, on them he bestows his farewell blessing; and plainly it is his love to Christ Himself that moves him to do so. Love to Him is the most essential mark of the children of God; and as this is an inward grace, an affection of the heart, it is plain that they are no outward body recognisable by men, but one that can be certainly known by God only. The last word, inadequately rendered in A. V. "in sincerity," and more exactly in R. V. "in uncorruptness," is peculiar. It is generally used in N. T. in connection with the eternal life and incorruptibility that is the heritage of the children of God, and not applied to moral qualities. The adjective is so applied in 1 Pet. iii. 4, and a cognate word is employed in Titus ii. 7 to describe the teaching of the Christian evangelist, as not to be perverted or silenced by any worldly motive. So here probably it denotes that Christian love should be not only sincere, or free from alloy of unworthy motives, but also constant, not to be overcome by any allurements, or quenched by any difficulties or dangers. Yet Paul plainly does not mean to describe any exceptional height of spiritual attainment, for that would limit in an unnatural way this most catholic prayer: what he describes he means as the common character of all true Christians, and he indicates that their love, though it must be ever growing, yet, if it be really genuine, has in it the germ of incorruptible life. For indeed it is that eternal life with which God has quickened us together with Christ. If it is indeed love to Jesus, the perfectly holy and loving One, the Christ, the Saviour sent and anointed by God, our Lord, who has made us His own by dying for us; as He can never change in those attributes that won our love at first, so He will not fail to keep our love for ever. Thus, while the blessing gives a high idea of what is implied in real discipleship, it is still most wide, embracing all of every nation and race, however much they may differ in belief or practice in many things, who are one in genuine love to our Lord Jesus Christ. This great blessing appropriately closes this great epistle.

THE END.

'These little books are models of the *multum in parvo* style. Little books on great subjects.'—*Literary World.*

Handbooks for Bible Classes
AND PRIVATE STUDENTS.
EDITED BY
PROF. MARCUS DODS, D.D., and ALEXANDER WHYTE, D.D.,
AND PUBLISHED BY
T. & T. CLARK, 38 GEORGE STREET, EDINBURGH.

In crown 8vo, price 2s.,

THE BOOK OF GENESIS.
With Introduction and Notes.
BY PROF. MARCUS DODS, D.D.

'Dr. Dods once more proves himself an able and accomplished biblical scholar; ... his Notes are the fruit of wide reading and earnest thought. They are pithy, scholarly, and suggestive—as weighty as they are brief.'—*Baptist Magazine.*

'Of the care with which the book has been done, and its thoroughness in every point, it is not possible to speak too highly.'—*Congregationalist.*

In Two Vols., crown 8vo, 2s. each,

THE BOOK OF EXODUS.
With Introduction, Commentary, Special Notes, Plans, etc.
BY THE LATE REV. JAMES MACGREGOR, D.D., OAMARU.

'The ablest and most compendious exposition of the Book of Exodus ever published in this country.'—*Methodist New Connexion Magazine.*

'This is an excellent manual. The Introduction is really a treatise, and would be valuable to readers of far higher pretensions than "Bible Classes"; and it is wonderfully cheap too.'—*Literary Churchman.*

In crown 8vo, price 1s. 6d.,

THE BOOK OF JOSHUA.
BY GEORGE C. M. DOUGLAS, D.D.,
PRINCIPAL OF THE FREE CHURCH COLLEGE, GLASGOW.

'I consider it a very valuable contribution to the full elucidation of one of the most interesting books in the Bible. Your treatment of each section is clear, simple, and intelligible to all readers. You have succeeded in shedding the light of modern travel and research upon the numerous topographical and historical details with which the writings of Joshua abound. I do not know any work of the same extent which possesses such an amount of valuable and trustworthy information. It is, in my opinion, a model "Handbook for Bible Classes."'—From Rev. President PORTER, D.D., Belfast.

Handbooks for Bible Classes
AND PRIVATE STUDENTS.

In crown 8vo, price 1s. 3d.,

THE BOOK OF JUDGES.
By GEORGE C. M. DOUGLAS, D.D.,
PRINCIPAL OF THE FREE CHURCH COLLEGE, GLASGOW.

'This volume is as near perfection as we can hope to find such a work.'—*Church Bells.*

In crown 8vo, price 1s. 6d.,

THE BOOKS OF CHRONICLES.
By JAMES G. MURPHY, LL.D., T.C.D.,
PROFESSOR OF HEBREW, BELFAST.

'Far beyond anything indicated by the small price of this work is its exceeding value for thoroughness of verbal exposition, exegetical criticism, and homiletic suggestiveness.'—*Baptist Magazine.*

In crown 8vo, price 1s. 6d.,

THE SIX INTERMEDIATE MINOR PROPHETS.
OBADIAH—ZEPHANIAH.
By Rev. Principal DOUGLAS, D.D., Glasgow.

'Introductions and notes are alike clear, compact, and suggestive.'—*Baptist Magazine.*

'Reverent, scholarly, comprehensive, and practical.'—*Christian.*

In crown 8vo, price 2s.,

THE POST-EXILIAN PROPHETS—
HAGGAI, ZECHARIAH, MALACHI.
By Professor MARCUS DODS, D.D.

'When the Books of the Old Testament are treated in this way, there is some hope that the standard of popular teaching will be sensibly raised. . . . We can only congratulate the rising generation in having guides like these.'—*Literary World.*

In crown 8vo, price 2s. 6d.,

THE GOSPEL ACCORDING TO ST. MARK.
With Introduction, Notes, and Maps.
By T. M. LINDSAY, M.A., D.D.,
PROF. OF DIVINITY AND CHURCH HISTORY, FREE CHURCH COLLEGE, GLASGOW.

'A careful commentary, and will be found most useful.'—*Spectator.*

'To say that this book is fully equal to all and any of those which have preceded it in the same series, is to give it high praise, but were we to say more even than that, we should not exaggerate. . . . There is a completeness about the work which gives it a peculiar value to the appreciative reader.'—*Christian.*

Handbooks for Bible Classes
AND PRIVATE STUDENTS.

In crown 8vo, Part I., price 2s.; Part II., price 1s. 3d.,
ST. LUKE'S GOSPEL.
With Introduction, Notes, and Maps.
By Professor T. M. LINDSAY, D.D.

'An admirable text-book, both for private aid and teaching purposes.'—*Spectator.*

'For point, clearness, freshness, and evangelical unction, they are not to be surpassed.'—*Young Men's Christian Magazine.*

In Two Vols., crown 8vo, 2s. each,
ST. JOHN'S GOSPEL.
With Introduction and Notes.
By Rev. GEORGE REITH, D.D., GLASGOW.

'The general excellence of the series is more than maintained. Indeed, for persons who require much in little, we can recommend nothing better than this unpretentious little work, in which the "Golden Gospel" is opened up with admirable conciseness and clearness.'—*The Christian.*

In Two Parts, crown 8vo, price 1s. 6d. each,
THE ACTS OF THE APOSTLES.
With Introduction, Notes, and Map.
By Professor T. M. LINDSAY, D.D.

'The largest and most pretentious books are not invariably the best. Frequently the value is in inverse ratio to the size, and this may certainly be affirmed of Dr. Lindsay's manual. It is of small bulk, but of great worth, giving us, in short compass, the best that has been thought and said in regard to the memorable section of Scripture with which it deals.'—*Baptist Magazine.*

In crown 8vo, price 2s.,
THE EPISTLE TO THE ROMANS.
By DAVID BROWN, D.D.,
PRINCIPAL, FREE CHURCH COLLEGE, ABERDEEN.

'We do not know a better book to recommend to Bible-class teachers or scholars in their study of this Epistle.'—*Glasgow Herald.*

In crown 8vo, price 1s. 6d.,
THE EPISTLE TO THE GALATIANS.
With Introduction and Notes.
By the late JAMES MACGREGOR, D.D., OAMARU.

'Sound, fresh, vigorous, readable, and learned, it opens up the Epistle in a way which makes its meaning plain to the commonest capacity. No minister lecturing through Galatians should be without it; and the teacher of a Bible class may now, with it in his hand, venture to take the Epistle as a text-book.'—*Free Church Record.*

Handbooks for Bible Classes
AND PRIVATE STUDENTS.

Just published, in crown 8vo, price 1s. 6d.,

THE EPISTLE TO THE EPHESIANS.
With Introduction and Notes.
By Professor J. S. CANDLISH, D.D.

In crown 8vo, price 2s. 6d.,

THE EPISTLE TO THE HEBREWS.
By A. B. DAVIDSON, D.D., LL.D.,
PROFESSOR OF HEBREW, ETC., NEW COLLEGE, EDINBURGH.

'The exposition is clear, helpful, and founded upon a painstaking study of the text and examination of the commentators.'—*English Churchman.*

In crown 8vo, price 1s. 6d.,

BISHOP BUTLER'S THREE SERMONS UPON HUMAN NATURE.
With Introduction and Notes.
By Rev. THOMAS B. KILPATRICK, B.D.

'Mr. Kilpatrick has written a decidedly able introduction, with valuable notes. His treatment of the aim of ethical study, and of the writings of British moralists, is clear, concise, and suitable.'—Prof. CALDERWOOD, LL.D.

'The best edition of the famous sermons that we have ever seen. No student of Butler should fail to procure it.'—*Literary World.*

In crown 8vo, price 2s.,

THE REFORMATION.
By T. M. LINDSAY, M.A., D.D.,
PROFESSOR OF DIVINITY AND CHURCH HISTORY, F. C. COLLEGE, GLASGOW.

'The best popular account we have yet seen of the causes, principles, and results of this momentous movement, whose main incidents it graphically describes. As a handbook the work is complete.'—*Baptist Magazine.*

In crown 8vo, Second Edition, price 2s.,

HISTORY OF THE IRISH PRESBYTERIAN CHURCH.
By President THOMAS HAMILTON, D.D., BELFAST.

'This is a most excellent handbook, and entirely worthy to take its place beside the other publications of the same series, all of which are written by distinguished men.... We see nothing but what is good and trustworthy in Mr. Hamilton's valuable book.'—*Belfast Northern Whig.*

Handbooks for Bible Classes
AND PRIVATE STUDENTS.

Just published, in crown 8vo, price 2s.,
THE LAST OF THE PROPHETS.
A Study of the Life, Teaching, and Character of
JOHN THE BAPTIST.
By Rev. J. FEATHER, Croydon.

In crown 8vo, price 2s.,
THE CHRISTIAN MIRACLES
AND THE CONCLUSIONS OF SCIENCE.
By Rev. W. D. THOMSON, M.A.

'This little volume has more real merit and is more really helpful than many large treatises.... An admirable little treatise, and one of the clearest and most sensible on the profound subjects on which it treats.'—*Christian Advocate.*

In crown 8vo, price 1s. 6d.,
SCOTTISH CHURCH HISTORY.
By NORMAN L. WALKER, D.D.

'This handbook will form an admirable basis for a course of instruction in Scottish ecclesiastical history.'—*British and Foreign Evangelical Review.*

'A very beautiful account of the history of Church matters in Scotland.... The utmost fairness and breadth characterises its treatment of questions and persons in opposition.'—*Presbyterian Churchman.*

In crown 8vo, price 1s. 6d.,
THE CHURCH.
By the late Professor WILLIAM BINNIE, D.D., Aberdeen.

'We commend this admirable handbook of Professor Binnie's to the notice of our friends, not only because they will find in it a clear statement and masterly vindication of Presbyterianism, but equally because they will learn much that may be of the highest and most practical advantage to themselves.'—*Baptist Magazine.*

In crown 8vo, Fourth Edition, with additional matter, price 2s. 6d.,
SHORT HISTORY OF CHRISTIAN MISSIONS,
From Abraham and Paul, to Carey, Libingstone, and Duff.
By GEORGE SMITH, LL.D., F.R.G.S., C.I.E.

'As a handbook of missionary history, the work is invaluable; while its style and fulness of instruction combine to give it the very foremost place among such works.'—*Sunday School Chronicle.*

Handbooks for Bible Classes
AND PRIVATE STUDENTS.

In crown 8vo, price 1s. 6d.,

THE CHRISTIAN DOCTRINE OF GOD.
By JAMES S. CANDLISH, D.D.,
PROFESSOR OF SYSTEMATIC THEOLOGY IN FREE CHURCH COLLEGE, GLASGOW.

'To have put all this deeply thought, richly furnished, and wisely expressed matter on the fundamental topic in theology within reach of the widest Christian public at the extremely modest cost named, must be pronounced a triumph of enterprise on the part of editors and publishers.'—*Theological Review.*

BY THE SAME AUTHOR.

In crown 8vo, price 1s. 6d.,

THE CHRISTIAN SACRAMENTS.

'An admirable manual; sound, clear, suggestive, and interesting.'—*Free Church Monthly.*

'It is just such a manual as ministers may with great advantage employ as a text-book in their Bible classes, and as intelligent youth (and intelligent old people too) may with great profit study for themselves.'—*British Messenger.*

BY THE SAME AUTHOR.

In crown 8vo, price 1s. 6d.,

THE WORK OF THE HOLY SPIRIT.

'A masterly, succinct, and suggestive *résumé* of the highest Christian thought on the personality and office of the Holy Spirit. A finer investigation of the teaching of Scripture, and a more luminous exhibition of its manifold relations to the origination and development of Christian character, we could not desire.'—*Baptist Magazine.*

BY THE SAME AUTHOR.

In crown 8vo, price 1s. 6d.,

THE BIBLICAL DOCTRINE OF SIN.

'What Professor Candlish has given us here in such admirable clearness and welcome brevity is the fruit of the most accomplished modern study.'—*Expository Times.*

Second Edition, Revised, in crown 8vo, price 3s.,

CHURCH AND STATE.
A Historical Handbook.
By A. TAYLOR INNES, Advocate.

'Our author, by his encyclopædic knowledge of the facts, his mastery of principles, his pellucid style, his charm of expression, enables one to trace the evolution of this intricate question with an ease that is fascinating.'—*The Critical Review.*

Handbooks for Bible Classes
AND PRIVATE STUDENTS.

Just published, in crown 8vo (with Map), price 2s.,
FROM THE EXILE TO THE ADVENT.
By Rev. WM. FAIRWEATHER, M.A.

Just published, Third Edition, Revised, in crown 8vo, price 2s. 6d.,
PALESTINE:
ITS HISTORICAL GEOGRAPHY.
With Topographical Index.
By ARCHIBALD HENDERSON, D.D.

With FIVE MAPS. The Maps have been specially revised by Major CONDER, R.E., of the Palestine Exploration Fund, for this Work.

'We cannot consider a Sunday-school teacher fully equipped without this volume.'—*Ecclesiastical Gazette.*

In crown 8vo, price 2s.,
THE WESTMINSTER CONFESSION OF FAITH.
With Introduction and Notes.
By Rev. J. MACPHERSON, M.A.

'This volume is executed with learning, discrimination, and ability.'—*British Messenger.*

'A work of great ability, giving a vast amount of information alike as to the history and meaning of that venerable Presbyterian symbol, and explaining its successive sections in the light of modern attacks upon its doctrine.'—*Young Men's Christian Magazine.*

BY THE SAME AUTHOR.
In crown 8vo, price 1s. 6d.,
PRESBYTERIANISM.

'A solid piece of workmanship, remarkable for the vast amount of information presented in a small compass, and so clearly set forth.'—*Christian Leader.*

BY THE SAME AUTHOR.
In crown 8vo, price 1s. 6d.,
THE SUM OF SAVING KNOWLEDGE.
With Introduction and Notes.

'We welcome this handbook. It is a singularly useful outline of Calvinistic doctrine, and will, we trust, be of much service to those who are willing to learn.'—*Sword and Trowel.*

'Cannot fail to be of the greatest utility where it is diligently used.'—*Clergyman's Magazine.*

'Read in the *Sum of Saving Knowledge*, the work which I think first of all wrought a saving change in me.'—*M'Cheyne's Diary.*

Handbooks for Bible Classes
AND PRIVATE STUDENTS.

In cr. 8vo, 1s. 6d.; or large-type Edition, handsomely bound, 3s. 6d.,

THE LIFE OF JESUS CHRIST.
By JAMES STALKER, D.D.

'As a succinct, suggestive, beautifully written exhibition of the Life of our Lord—so far as we know it and can form a conception of it—we are acquainted with nothing that can compare with it. . . . It is in its way a gem; and none who read it thoughtfully can fail to appreciate its worth.'—*Christian World.*

'No work since "Ecce Homo" has at all approached this in succinct, clear-cut, and incisive criticism on Christ as He appeared to those who believed in Him.'—*Literary World.*

BY THE SAME AUTHOR.

In cr. 8vo, 1s. 6d.; or large-type Edition, handsomely bound, 3s. 6d.,

THE LIFE OF ST. PAUL.

'Even to those who know by heart the details of the great Apostle's life, this glowing sketch will be a revelation. Written with a fine sympathy for the more tender and personal aspects of his theme, Mr. Stalker has portrayed the outer and the inner life of Paul with a mingled power and beauty which is as rare as it is needed in evangelical writing.'—*Christian.*

'Mr. Stalker has the gift of vivid writing; he sketches and colours with words; he does more, he vivifies persons and scenes by his inspiring sentences. We have not often seen a handbook more completely to our mind.'—C. H. SPURGEON.

'A gem of sacred biography.'—*Christian Leader.*

In crown 8vo, price 2s. 6d.,

LESSONS ON THE LIFE OF JESUS.
By Rev. WILLIAM SCRYMGEOUR, M.A.

'Extremely good, and will be found very useful by Sunday-school teachers, and others who may not have time to read larger books.'—*Church Bells.*

'Among the many books on the life of our Lord which have issued from the press of late years, this handbook will take a definite place. . . . Students and teachers will find it a reliable volume.'—*Watchman.*

In crown 8vo, price 2s. 6d.,

A COMMENTARY ON THE SHORTER CATECHISM.
By ALEXANDER WHYTE, D.D.,
FREE ST. GEORGE'S, EDINBURGH.

'Really good. In every Scotch family this ought to be found. Our English folk are not so well acquainted with "The Shorter Catechism"; but those who are will be glad to have a handbook upon it, so clear, so true, and so lively. . . . Theology of this stamp will do us all good. Scatter it; its leaves are for the healing of the nations. Half-a-crown laid out in this book will purchase no regrets.'—Mr. SPURGEON.

HOW TO READ THE PROPHETS:

Being the Prophecies arranged Chronologically in their Historical Setting, with Explanations, Maps, and Glossary.

BY REV. BUCHANAN BLAKE, B.D.

Now Complete, in Five Volumes Crown 8vo.

Part I. THE PRE-EXILIAN MINOR PROPHETS (with JOEL). *Second Edition.* Price 4s.
Part II. ISAIAH (Chapters i.-xxxix.). *Second Edition.* Price 2s. 6d.
Part III. JEREMIAH. Price 4s.
Part IV. EZEKIEL. Price 4s.
Part V. ISAIAH (xl.-lxvi.) and THE POST-EXILIAN PROPHETS. Price 4s.

"*It has often been found a difficulty to profit fully from the reading, especially of the smaller prophecies of the Old Testament. To make these prophecies intelligible to the plainest reader, it seems desirable that a chronological arrangement of the prophetic books should be attempted. Alongside of the several prophecies should be placed those portions of the Old Testament historical books which deal with the same period. The aim of these manuals is consequently in this direction: to bring within the reach of the many a clear and succinct presentation of these prophets in their historical environment.*"—From the AUTHOR'S INTRODUCTION.

"So far as Mr Blake's series has gone it is unrivalled."—*The Sunday School.*

"Those who already possess the earlier parts of the same work will at once possess themselves of this new volume. Those who do not, will be glad to have it recommended to their notice. The author's plan has grown since he first announced it, and we are glad of it, as the treatment is more full and thorough. It is enough now to say that there is nothing like this little book on Jeremiah."—*Church Bells.*

"Mr Blake has already taught us how to read Isaiah and the Minor Prophets, and we have found the task much lightened in consequence, scarcely any more a toilsome task at all. For the difficulty of the Prophets is in their arrangement, together with the numerous allusions, local and historical, and these are the things Mr Blake takes pains to put right for us. He puts them right, so that now we stand, as far as it is possible we ever could stand, in the same position as the prophet's hearers. No 'Aids to the Study of the Bible' can approach these in real helpfulness for the ordinary Bible reader."—*The Expository Times.*

"A pleasure to read, and profit for the reading. . . . The arrangement of the historical sections, and the prophetical utterances connected therewith, is admirable. All Bible students have reason to be grateful to the author for this entertaining volume; its form is inviting, its interest absorbing."—*Church Times.*

"A well-conceived and carefully executed attempt to make these writings speak for themselves. . . . His book will give a new meaning to these prophecies to many a reader."—*The Critical Review.*

EDINBURGH: T. & T. CLARK, 38 GEORGE STREET.
LONDON: SIMPKIN, MARSHALL, HAMILTON, KENT & CO., LTD.

'A most useful series of Handbooks. With such helps as these, to be an inefficient teacher is to be blameworthy.'—Rev. C. H. SPURGEON.

BIBLE CLASS PRIMERS.

Edited by Rev. Professor SALMOND, D.D.

In paper covers, 6d. each; free by post, 7d. In cloth, 8d. each; free by post, 9d.

The Making of Israel. By Rev. C. A. SCOTT, B.D.
The Truth of Christianity. By Rev. Professor IVERACH, D.D.
The Sabbath. By Rev. Professor SALMOND, D.D.
Our Christian Passover. By Rev. C. A. SALMOND, M.A.
The Kingdom of God. A Plan of Study. In Three Parts. By Rev. F. HERBERT STEAD, M.A.
The Parables of Our Lord. By Rev. Professor SALMOND, D.D.
Life of St. John. By PATON J. GLOAG, D.D.
Life of Abraham. By Rev. C. A. SCOTT, B.A.
Historical Connection between the Old and New Testaments. By Rev. JOHN SKINNER, M.A.
The Life of Christ. By Rev. Professor SALMOND, D.D.
The Shorter Catechism. In Three Parts. By Rev. Prof. SALMOND, D.D.
The Period of the Judges. By the Rev. Professor PATERSON, M.A., Edinburgh.
Outlines of Protestant Missions. By JOHN ROBSON, D.D.
Life of the Apostle Peter. By Rev. Professor SALMOND, D.D.
Outlines of Early Church History. By the late Rev. HENRY WALLIS SMITH, D.D.
  'An admirable sketch of early Church history.'—*Baptist.*
Life of David. By the late Rev. PETER THOMSON, M.A.
Life of Moses. By Rev. Professor IVERACH, D.D.
  'Accurately done, clear, mature, and scholarly.'—*Christian.*
Life of Paul. By PATON J. GLOAG, D.D.
  'This little book could not well be surpassed.'—*Daily Review.*
Life and Reign of Solomon. By Rev. RAYNER WINTERBOTHAM, M.A., LL.B.
  'Every teacher should have it.'—Rev. C. H. SPURGEON.
The History of the Reformation. By Rev. Professor WITHEROW.
  'A vast amount of information set forth in a clear and concise manner.'—*United Presbyterian Magazine.*
The Kings of Israel. By Rev. W. WALKER, M.A.
  'A masterpiece of lucid condensation.'—*Christian Leader.*
The Kings of Judah. By Rev. Professor GIVEN, Ph.D.
  'Admirably arranged; the style is sufficiently simple and clear to be quite within the compass of young people.'—*British Messenger.*
Joshua and the Conquest. By Rev. Professor CROSKERY.
  'This carefully written manual will be much appreciated.'—*Daily Review.*

Bible Words and Phrases, Explained and Illustrated. By Rev. CHARLES MICHIE, M.A. 18mo, cloth, 1s.
  'Will be found interesting and instructive, and of the greatest value to young students and teachers.'—*Athenæum.*
The Seven Churches of Asia. By DEBORAH ALCOCK. 18mo, cl., 1s.

T. and T. Clark's Publications.

A NEW AND CHEAPER EDITION.

In crown 8vo, Third Edition, price 3s. 6d.,

BEYOND THE STARS;

OR,

Heaven, Its Inhabitants, Occupations, and Life.

By THOMAS HAMILTON, D.D.,

PRESIDENT OF QUEEN'S COLLEGE, BELFAST;
AUTHOR OF 'HISTORY OF THE IRISH PRESBYTERIAN CHURCH,' ETC. ETC.

CONTENTS:—Chap. I. Introductory.—II. A Settling of Localities.—III. God.—IV. The Cherubim.—V. The Angels.—VI. The Saints.—VII. Children in Heaven.—VIII. Do they know one another in Heaven?—IX. Common Objections to the Doctrine of Recognition in Heaven.—X. Between Death and the Resurrection.—XI. How to get there.

PRESS NOTICES.

'A good book upon a grand subject. . . . His writing is solid, he dissipates dreams, but he establishes authorised hopes. . . . This is a book which a believer will enjoy all the more when he draws nearer to those blessed fields "beyond the stars."'—Mr. Spurgeon in *Sword and Trowel.*

'The work of a man of strong sense and great power of lucid thought and expression, one who has deep springs of tenderness. He puts himself well in touch with his audience, and arranges what he has to say in the clearest manner.'—*British Weekly.*

'The author's natural and sympathetic eloquence lends at times a brightness, and again a more pathetic charm, to his theme. We cannot doubt that his book will comfort as well as interest a wide circle of readers.'—*Scottish Leader.*

'Many a bruised heart will be made joyful on reading this book. . . . On a former occasion, when reviewing a book by the same author, we congratulated the Irish Presbyterian Church on having among her younger ministers a writer of such promise and power. We believe we may now congratulate the wider Christian Church on a teacher and guide whose words will fortify and cheer wherever the English language is spoken.'—*Presbyterian Messenger.*

'There is not a dry or uninteresting page in it, and most of the chapters are profoundly absorbing in their style and matter. It reads like a novel, yet there is nothing mawkish or sentimental about it; but it is reverent, devout, frank, manly, and orthodox in its tone and character.'—*Christian Advocate.*

'The tone is reverent, the style is clear, the reasoning is careful. Its capital type will recommend it to the weary sight of some to whom the "land of distances" is no longer the land that is very far off.'—*Church Bells.*

'Dr. Hamilton endeavours to tell in plain and popular language all that the Bible reveals about the other life. The tone of the book is admirable; devout and modest throughout.'—*London Quarterly Review.*

Annual Volumes, in cloth binding, price 7s. 6d.
Published Monthly, price 6d. Annual (prepaid) Subscription, 6s.

THE EXPOSITORY TIMES.
EDITED BY REV. JAMES HASTINGS, M.A.

N.B.—**A New Volume commences with each October Issue.**

'Any student of theology, still more anyone who has a spiritual charge, will find much that is profitable in the Magazine.'—*The Spectator*.

'A truly valuable publication.'—*Independent*.

'We cordially commend the Magazine to all students of modern theology.—*Church Bells*.

'THE EXPOSITORY TIMES grows upon its readers, and is looked for eagerly month by month.'—*Methodist Recorder*.

'Whoever wishes the latest and best thought on biblical criticism, archæology, and exposition, will find it here.'—*Literary World*.

'The fifth volume of THE EXPOSITORY TIMES is to hand. To say of it that it will compare favourably with any of its predecessors, is to say much. The Editor's own work is always done with taste and point, and he has the assistance of many competent writers. Some of the papers, especially those on the Theology of Isaiah, by Professor A. B. Davidson, stand out conspicuous. But there are others, too many to particularise, which make interesting contributions to a wide variety of subjects—the interpretation of difficult texts, the estimate of notable theologians, the study of the Prophets, the criticism of the Gospels, and others.' The needs of the busy minister are a special subject of consideration in this valuable magazine.'—*Critical Review*.

Now ready, in cloth binding, price 7s., Volume V. of

THE CRITICAL REVIEW.
EDITED BY PROF. S. D. F. SALMOND, D.D.

Containing *signed* REVIEWS of all the important Theological and Philosophical Books published during the past year, and NOTICES and RECORD OF SELECT LITERATURE, by the Editor.

Published Quarterly, price 1s. 6d. Annual (prepaid) Subscription, 6s.

'This volume surpasses, if that be possible, in the quality of its contents, the previous issues, and that indeed is high praise. . . . The important books of the year are criticised by competent hands. . . . The short notices of books by the Editor are always pithy and pregnant. The Record of Select Literature, at the end of each number, is a valuable conspectus of the latest books. . . . Theological students who desire to be abreast of the theological movements in England, America, and the Continent, cannot do better than read this thoroughly high-class review.'—*Christian World*.

'Indispensable as a guide to modern theological thought and literature.'—*Church Bells*.

'THE CRITICAL REVIEW has established its claim to be an indispensable guide to the chief theological and philosophical literature of the day. It is not possible to find anywhere else a series of brief notices so adequately descriptive yet so full of sound criticism as these. . . . Dr. Salmond has a splendid set of helpers, and the value of THE CRITICAL REVIEW is becoming more and more evident.'—*London Quarterly*.

www.ingramcontent.com/pod-product-compliance
Lightning Source LLC
Chambersburg PA
CBHW031323160426
43196CB00007B/639